ETHIOPIA
THE ROOF OF AFRICA

DISCOVERING our HERITAGE

by Jane Kurtz

dP| **DILLON PRESS**
New York

Maxwell Macmillan Canada
Toronto

Maxwell Macmillan International
New York Oxford Singapore Sydney

To my family, who, in good
Ethiopian tradition, made this a family project.

Acknowledgments

The author would like to thank the following people and organizations for their assistance with the text and/or photographs: the Ethiopian Embassy, the Ethiopian Tourist Organization, Friends of Ethiopia, Jay Hauger, Caroline Kurtz, Chris Kurtz, Harold and Polly Kurtz, and Geri and Tasissa Moti.

Library of Congress Cataloging-in-Publication Data

Kurtz, Jane.
Ethiopia : the roof of Africa / by Jane Kurtz.
   p. cm. —(Discovering our heritage)
Includes bibliographical references and index.
   Summary: Describes the geography, history, culture, economy, and people of the mountainous country in northeastern Africa troubled in recent years by drought, famine, and civil unrest.
ISBN: 0-87518-483-9
1. Ethiopia—Juvenile literature. [1. Ethiopia.] I. Title.
II. Series.
DT373.K78 1991
963—dc20

91-18660

Dillon Press
Macmillan Publishing Company
866 Third Avenue
New York, NY 10022
Maxwell Macmillan Canada, Inc.
1200 Eglinton Avenue East
Suite 200
Don Mills, Ontario M3C 3N1
Macmillan Publishing Company is part of the Maxwell Communication Group of Companies.
First edition
Printed in the United States of America
10   9   8   7   6   5   4   3   2   1

Contents

Fast Facts about Ethiopia

Official Name: *Ethiopia.*
Capital: Addis Ababa.
Location: East Africa. Sudan lies on the western side of the triangle, Kenya lies on the southern side, Somalia, Djibouti and the coast of the Red Sea lie along the northeastern side.
Area: 476,834 square miles (1,235,000 square kilometers). *Greatest Distances:* North-South—1552.5 miles (2,500 kilometers); east-west—1490.4 miles (800 kilometers).
Elevation: *Highest*—(Mt. Ras Deshen) 15,158 feet (4,620 meters) above sea level. *Lowest*—426.4 feet (130 meters) below sea level.
Population: 52,000,000 (1991). *Distribution*—10 percent urban, 90 percent rural. *Density*—69 persons per square mile (26 persons per square kilometer).
Form of Government: The Transitional Government of Ethiopia.
Important Products: *Agriculture*—coffee, cattle, cotton. *Industry*—cottage crafts, Ethiopian Airlines, a handful of small factories.
Basic Unit of Money: Birr.

Major Languages: Amharic, Tigrinya, Oromifa, English.
Major Religions: Orthodox Christian and Muslim.
Flag: Three horizontal stripes in green, yellow, and red.
National Anthem: *National Anthem of Ethiopia* (being changed).
Major Holidays: Ethiopian Christmas (*Ganna*)—January 7; Ethiopian Epiphany (*Timket*)—January 19; Adua Day—March 2; Good Friday, Easter, Ramadan; New Year's Day—September 11; Revolution Day—September 12; Finding of the True Cross (*Maskal*)—September 27, Arafa.

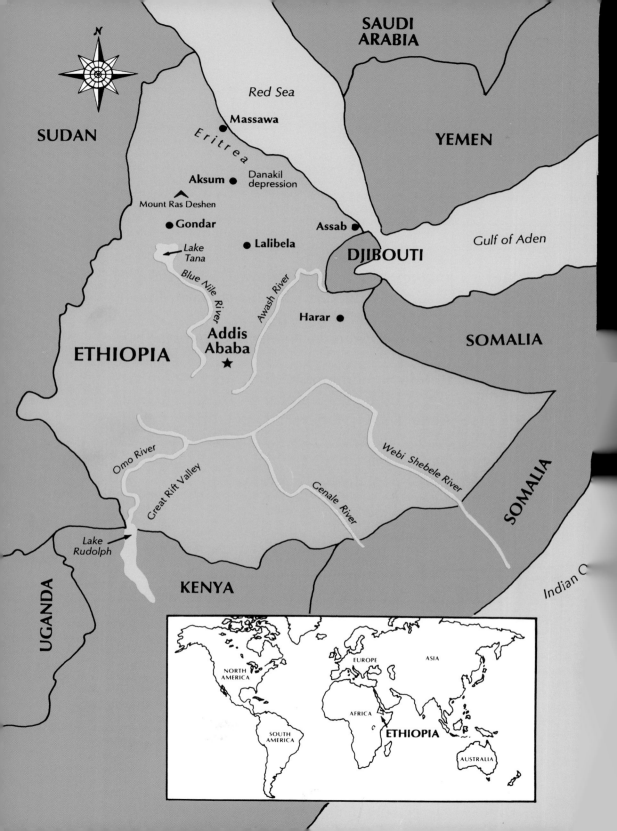

1. A High Mountain Fortress

Ethiopia is a country of contrasts. It is a country where millions of people face starvation because of severe droughts and civil war that tore apart the northern region for more than thirty years. Yet the stories of kings and castles, of farmers and nomads, are as much a part of this diverse African nation as famine and war. Inhabitants of southern and central Ethiopia were seldom touched by the war. People in the rural southern and central parts of Ethiopia, far from the troubled north, still live in small villages or out on the plains with their families, their farms, their animals, their music and dancing, just as they have always done.

If you look at a map of Africa, you can easily identify the part called "the horn" on the western coast, near the Middle East. Ethiopia is located on the Horn of Africa. Shaped like a triangle, the country is about the size of Texas, Oklahoma, and New Mexico put together. To the northeast is the Red Sea, across which lie the Arabian countries of Yemen and Saudi Arabia. To the west and south lie the African countries of Sudan and Kenya, respectively. Because of its neighbors, Ethiopia is a country with both an African and an Arabian flavor.

Called "the Roof of Africa," Ethiopia has more high

Ehiopia is often called the "Roof of Africa" because so much of the country sits on a high plateau.

ground than any other country on the continent. Two-thirds of the country rests on a high plateau, split by the Great Rift Valley that runs from the Red Sea down into central Africa. But the land also plunges to desert lands 426 feet (130 meters) below sea level.

On top of the Ethiopian plateau, there are jagged river valleys, 15,000-foot (4,572-meter) high mountains, and the 10-mile (16-kilometer) wide Blue Nile gorge. To reach the plateau from the flat plains, a traveler has to climb a sheer rock face 6,000 feet (1,829 meters) high in places.

This high, rugged land kept Ethiopia from being conquered by other civilizations throughout the ages. While European countries were colonizing the rest of Africa, Ethiopians retreated into their highlands and fought off invasion. Except for five years during World War II, Ethiopia—unlike any other African country—remained independent.

A Communication Problem

Ethiopia's geography, which protected it from invading neighbors, turned into a barrier when the time came to develop communication, travel, and trade with neighbors and within the country. The forbidding geography created problems that Ethiopia is still trying to overcome.

In many countries, rivers are highways for travel and commerce. But only one of Ethiopia's large rivers, the Genale, reaches the sea. The Blue Nile tumbles out of Lake Tana, then flows west into the White Nile as its waters move to Sudan and Egypt. The Omo River flows south into Lake Rudolf (most of which lies in Kenya), and the Webi Shebele River runs east to Somalia. The Baraka River flows north toward the Red Sea but loses itself in the sand before getting there. The Awash River winds north through the Great Rift Valley, but then sinks into the Danakil depression, a basin in the northeastern corner of Ethiopia.

Rivers more often divided rather than connected the land and its people. For a long time, people identified themselves with the nearest river and considered people on the other side of the river as alien. Since the rivers flow down from highlands, they often drop into rapids or long waterfalls, making boat travel impossible. Boats can navigate the Blue Nile as far as Gambela, just over the Sudan border, but then the river climbs and is full of waterfalls, including the spectacular *Tississat* (smoke of fire) where thundering falls create a mist that looks like smoke. During the dry season, rivers are too low for travel, and during the rainy season, river currents are too fast and dangerous. River valleys tend to be hot, full of mosquitoes carrying malaria and other diseases, so they became places for *shiftas* (outlaws) to hide.

Ethiopia couldn't count on roads, either. Although wheels were developed in the ancient Ethiopian civilization of Aksum, their use died out because donkeys and mules were more surefooted on steep mountain trails. For many years, the country had hardly any roads and only one short railroad line.

A Varied and Startling Land

The mountainous Ethiopian highlands were once covered by dense forests. But today only about 5 percent of the country, mostly in the southwest, has thick trees. In most

The many rivers that flow from the highlands produce spectacular waterfalls as they descend into the valleys.

Once able to support many forests, much of Ethiopia is now covered by dry savanna grasslands.

other parts of the country, savanna grasslands (bushes and occasional trees) have replaced forests. Early Ethiopians viewed trees as a gift from God, not as a resource that they needed to replace. Thousands of trees were chopped down for firewood and farming. In the nineteenth century, however, one of Ethiopia's emperors imported eucalyptus trees from Australia. Around the capital city of Addis Ababa, and even in many villages, slender eucalyptus trees with their blue-gray leaves and sharp scent are the most common kind of tree today.

Because Ethiopia is only a few degrees north of the

equator, the high plateau has a mild climate. During the dry season, days are warm and bright. Even during the "little rains" (between March and June) and the "big rains" (mid-June to September), the sun usually shines sometime during the day, giving the Ethiopian Tourist Organization its slogan: Thirteen Months of Sunshine.

Where the plateau drops into flatlands, Ethiopia is hot and dry. In some places near the Red Sea, rain never falls. The Red Sea ports of Massawa and Assab are among the hottest places on earth.

One of the strangest places in Ethiopia is the Danakil depression. Here, mountains end in a sandy desert where volcanic cones poke through the sand. Salty flats of dried-up inland seas about 400 feet (122 meters) below sea level are scattered throughout the sand. Temperatures can rise to 120°F in the Danakil desert. Hot springs bubble through sand that is colored orange, yellow, green, and blue in places from natural chemical deposits. Clustered around the springs are geometric salt castles, built from tiny, perfect cubes of salt left by the water, piling up on one another.

Ethiopia's varied geography is home to many interesting and colorful animals. The plains rumble with the world's largest herds of elands (large antelopes) and smaller bands of elephants. Wild pigs snort through the grasses where zebras, antelopes, and giraffes graze, keeping a watch out for prides of lions. Oryxes toss their

The various habitats of Ethiopia are home to many different kinds of animals, including these giraffes.

horns, and ostriches flap awkwardly away. In rivers and ponds, hippopotamuses and crocodiles yawn. White and black colobus monkeys and baboons fling themselves from tree to tree deep in the forests. In the south-central part of the country, Bale National Park protects the home of the mountain nyala and Simien fox, found only in Ethiopia. On the northern lakes of the Great Rift Valley, clouds of pink flamingos cover the water. Even in cities, people can hear whooping hyenas at night.

More than one million people live in the crowded city of Addis Ababa, Ethiopia's capital.

A Crowded Capital

Though most people still live in the countryside, Ethiopia has at least two million urban people. Most of them live in the capital city of Addis Ababa, located in the middle of the country. Over a million people crowd the city, trying to find housing and work. Young people in Addis Ababa often put off marriage because of the housing shortage. Some have been looking for jobs for a year or more.

In the heart of the city stands Revolution Square, a huge and bustling open-air parade ground designed for great parades and demonstrations. Tall, modern buildings such as City Hall, Addis Ababa University, Black Lion Hospital, and various hotels, restaurants, and foreign embassies stand beside shacks of rust and mud.

In Addis Ababa, life and traffic move quickly. Streets stream with little blue-and-white Fiat taxis, red-and-yellow buses, and newer taxis with seats that face each other in back. People call the new taxis *we-et* (discussion) because you can discuss things with the other people as you drive along. By way of contrast, donkeys trot down the middle of side streets, dropping bits of hay from huge loads on their backs.

The sidewalks are free of trash, but homeless children beg for coins or food from passers-by. Many crippled people also make their living on the sidewalks. Extended families crowd into two-room houses made of sheet metal, mud, and stones propped like dominoes against each other. There is no electricity or running water in these houses. The family's one bed is often in the kitchen (a small kerosene stove and pots and pans often hang on the walls).

Shoppers can buy goods at small stores, but the imported things are all expensive. Instead, most people

Most Ethiopians do their shopping at the local markato, *a market where vendors sell fruits, vegetables, and other everyday items.*

go to the *markato*, or market, just as they would in any village. There they can buy food, clothes, and household supplies. The markato is crammed with people, and the smells of coffee, incense, garlic, ginger, people, and animals fill the air. At the edge along one sidewalk, sewing machines click and whir in a line as tailors sew clothes. Closer to the center, the ground is a quilt of bright, hot spices where women sit beside their ginger, onions, and hot peppers. People stop to buy cottage cheese or butter wrapped in leaves. In two big central buildings, young boys coax and call, trying to get people to look at their souvenirs.

A few other cities dot the countryside. The ancient walled city of Harar, once a city-state with its own government, has beautiful markets. Outside the railroad city of Dire Dawa, camel trains plod. The hot port city of Massawa on the Red Sea dates from the Middle Ages. Three old cities remain where ancient kingdoms were centered in northern Ethiopia: Aksum, Lalibela, and Gondar. In Aksum—once the greatest and most powerful city between the Roman Empire and Persia—ruined buildings and tall obelisks (decorated pillars) still stand. The next great capital city in Ethiopia's history was Lalibela with its eleven huge churches, each carved from pieces of solid rock, some connected by tunnels. Gondar, which came to power after Lalibela, is filled with the stone castles of ancient emperors.

Dramatic Changes and Hard Times

For centuries, Ethiopia was ruled by kings who traced their ancestry back to King Solomon of the Bible. But in 1974, the time of the kings ended for Ethiopia. The communist revolution deposed the last emperor, Haile Selassie, and a provisional military administrative council called the *Derg*, or committee, was set up to rule the country.

In 1975, the government organized all urban areas into *kebeles,* or neighborhood associations, which make political and administrative decisions for the neighborhoods. There are two to five hundred households to a kebele.

Between 1974 and 1991, Ethiopians saw some changes, but they also saw cruelty and many policies that took away basic human rights and made life even harder than it was before the revolution. The people of Ethiopia still did not have freedom of speech, assembly, or travel. For many who dreamed of better days, the dreams, hopes, and hard work continue.

In the spring of 1991, a coalition of groups overthrew the Communist government. They set up a transitional government and promised to work toward democracy and a system that would represent all ethnic groups.

A Mosaic of Different Peoples

In 1987, the *Shengo* identified twenty-nine different regions in Ethiopia. Many different ethnic groups are spread across those regions. In many cases, they are so different that the only thing that ties them together is that they are all Ethiopians. They have different clothing, religions, histories, and customs. The biggest group, the

Oromo (twenty-nine million), were dominated for hundreds of years by Amhara-Tigre culture (three to four million people).

Because of conflicts among the Oromo, Tigre, Eritrean, and Amhara people, language is a big issue in Ethiopia today. Though there are at least seventy or eighty different languages in the country, two-thirds of the people speak either Oromifa, *Amharic*, or *Tigrinya* at home. While the Amhara ruled Ethiopia until 1974, government officials and most landlords were Amhara, and the official language of Ethiopia was Amharic. Other ethnic groups could not use their languages in public places. After the revolution, newspapers and radios added other languages, but the working language of the government was still Amharic (with English as a second choice) and language policy continued to divide people.

For a short time after the 1974 revolution, non-Amhara groups thought they would be treated fairly. In the beginning, all major ethnic groups were represented in the Derg. But, as the new government developed, power stayed mostly in the hands of the Amhara. In response, some ethnic groups organized to fight the central government. The Tigrean People's Liberation Front liberated the northern Tigre region and made its own social changes. Its goal was not independence from Ethiopia, but for Ethiopia to be a democratic country where all Ethiopians would have basic freedoms and a real voice in the government. The Oromo and six or seven other groups had also launched resistance movements.

Eritrea—At War with the Rest of Ethiopia

In the northern part of the country is the region of *Eritrea*, a region that was at war with the rest of Ethiopia. Situated on the Red Sea, Eritrea was once an independent country that became an Italian colony. After World War II, the United Nations federated it with Ethiopia, but Eritrea was allowed to keep its own parliament. Ten years later, Ethiopia made the territory just another province, and the people were forced to give up their flag and to use the Amharic language. At that time, the rebellion against Ethiopia began. For thirty years, the Eritrean Liberation Front (ELF) fought to become an independent nation.

Fearing the loss of shipping if it lost its Red Sea ports, Ethiopia fought back with one of the largest armies on the African continent, including whole divisions of boys as young as thirteen. About half the national budget was spent on the army, although the money was desperately needed for economic development.

Eritrea was once thick with forests and wild animals. The people cut down the forests, and for a while it was a land with cotton fields and farms and a few cities scattered along the coast. Now, drought and erosion have made it a land of dust.

The loss of good farmland would have caused problems with food production even if the Eritrean people were not fighting a war for independence. The war only made food shortages worse. People could not plant while they were running from war, and fighting often blocked supplies for people whose crops failed. Now that the war is over, the northern part of the country will still need to help millions of starving people get food and start life over as farmers again.

Economic Hard Times

Experts call Ethiopia the poorest country in the world. Most people make their living through farming and few earn even $100 per year. Some machine-operated state-owned farms were organized after 1974, but many farmers still use simple plows—drawn by oxen or by the farmers themselves—and other methods that haven't changed for centuries.

The communist government started peasants' associations to help improve farming methods, but most peasants did not accept them, seeing them as a way for the government to tell them what to do rather than organizations that would help them. When that government fell apart, the state farms and whole villages broke apart and people quickly went back to farming the way they wanted. Small towns began to bustle with

The majority of Ethiopians earn a living by farming—a way of life that is becoming more difficult because of drought and soil depletion.

private trade as farmers, no longer forced to deliver food for low prices, began to rebuild their lives.

Along with grain and vegetables for their own use, farmers grow coffee to export. Coffee, which Ethiopians claim was named after the Kaffa province in Ethiopia where it grows wild, accounts for 70 percent of Ethiopia's export earnings. Even with collective farms, 97 percent of the coffee is grown by independent farmers.

In the north, farmers are even poorer than the rest of the country. For centuries, farmers there had to give half of their crops to landlords, 25 percent in tax to the government, and 10 percent to the church. Since they could use or sell only 15 percent of what they grew, even one bad season could ruin a farmer. People had to work the land as hard as possible to make a living. They were not motivated to look ahead and take good care of land they did not own. Erosion spoiled much of the countryside. Now, in years when the rains don't come and harvests are bad, farmers need tons of outside food to keep them from starving.

Drought years used to happen about once every ten years. Between 1973-1974, tens of thousands of people died in Tigre and Wallo provinces. Between 1984-1985, about a million people starved, including people in the western provinces where there was no drought but where harsh government policies made it hard for farmers to make a living. Lately, the country has had increasingly less rain. But in years when the rain falls, only pockets of starvation remain.

Isolation and independence have shaped Ethiopian history, character, music, politics, and economy. For most African countries, traditional values and ways of life began to splinter when the country was colonized. In Ethiopia, however, the old way of life began to change only recently. Ethiopia is now in the middle of an intense struggle to deal with those changes and to unite the country into one peaceful, connected nation.

Even in these troubled times, Ethiopians tend to meet immense hardships with grace and an accepting attitude. Many Ethiopians believe that their independence, their fierce love of their country, and their hopes for their children will eventually make Ethiopia a good home for all of its people.

2. Celebration in the Middle of Hardship

What does it mean to be an Ethiopian? Most people who come from Eritrea don't consider themselves to be Ethiopians. The hunters and gatherers on the plains, who still live like their earliest ancestors, don't have any concept of being part of a nation. No one custom, religion, language, or music is shared by all Ethiopians.

Over the years, as different ethnic groups traded at each other's markets, intermarried, and borrowed each other's customs, they gradually became connected. While each group has kept its own flavor, they do share some traits. Almost all Ethiopians know how to celebrate in the midst of hardship, and they love wit and good conversation. They also tend to admire physical courage, even aggression. In the past, each group produced fierce warriors. In fact, the Tigre, Amhara, Oromo, and Eritreans have a long history of battles with one another.

Ethnic Divisions

The Tigre is the smallest of the major groups, making up about 8 percent of the population. Tigre and Amhara people share a Semitic cultural heritage and together shaped Ethiopian culture and politics. But the Tigre consider themselves purer descendants of Ethiopia's first great kingdom. Their language is closest to the ancient language of *Geez* and, traditionally, the Tigre upheld Ethiopian Christianity in its purest form. They speak Tigrinya and live in the northern area where their ancestors migrated from Arabia, intermarried with Agew people, and established the capital city of Aksum.

The Amhara probably came from the area just to the south of Aksum. Their ancestors were a proud and warlike people, and after A.D. 1270, all emperors of Ethiopia except one were Amhara. Even before Amharic became the official language of Ethiopia, it was called *lesana negos* (the language of the king) and was spoken for centuries by almost everybody on the central plateau. Throughout history, the Amhara were strongly loyal to Ethiopian Christianity. Though comprising only about one quarter of the population, they had a strong sense of Amhara superiority, and spread their ways and attitudes throughout the country which they (together with the Tigre) dominated for centuries.

The Oromo, about 60 percent of the population, can be found in every Ethiopian province except two, but live mostly in central, southern, and southwestern Ethiopia. In the sixteenth and seventeenth centuries, Oromo groups began to fight their way onto the plateau, adopting their neighbors' customs wherever they settled. Those close to Muslim groups adopted Islam and those near the Ethiopian

Christian communities adopted Orthodox Christianity. As a result, each Oromo group has a different history, culture, and language.

Eritrea, the northernmost region, has nine different ethnic groups that speak many different languages. Some speak Tigre—a language descended from Tigrinya that has become so different it can no longer be understood by the Tigre people who speak the present Tigrinya! What holds them together is their sense of national identity. Eritreans are committed and resourceful. In spite of great danger and hardship, they managed to create a somewhat normal life for themselves. Until recently, anyone thirty years old and younger has never known life without war.

Smaller tribes have their special ways, too. The Guraghe, a Semitic tribe from the highlands, are considered the hardest workers, willing to take on any task. The Afar who live in the Danakil desert tend to be fierce, unfriendly to strangers. The Nuer, a people who live on the southern plains, organize their lives around herds of cattle. The many other tribes all have their own customs.

Today the Amhara, Tigre, and Oromo all dress alike and share many beliefs and attitudes. But sharp differences still exist. Oromo tend to meet each other as equals. They did not traditionally have a drive to gain power over others. An Amharic proverb, on the other hand, says, "*Amara yazzal inji aytazzezim*" ("the Amhara is to rule, not to be ruled").

The people that live in the highlands of Ethiopia build simple mud houses with roofs made of grass.

Life in the Regions of Ethiopia

On the plains of Ethiopia, most people are nomads. Some tribes own very little and simply hunt and gather food wherever they can find it. Others travel with herds of cattle, sheep, goats, or camels, setting up a temporary settlement when they find a good place for food and water. They live in houses made from animal skins or river grass, which can be taken down quickly and easily put up in another place. Particularly along the Baro River—which in recent years has suffered floods that washed many homes away—some tribes have started to settle down in villages, using river water to grow crops.

The southern and middle highlands are warm during the day, cold at night. The land is wonderfully green most of the year, with trees and bushes. People tend their little farms and animals, or hike to and from larger fields.

People live in round houses made of mud with roofs of grass or sometimes tin. Their houses are grouped together with four or five other houses or in larger villages around productive farmland. Inside each house is a fire with stones around it for cooking food, a place for each family member to sleep, and sometimes a place for the family's animals. Traditional clothes are made of white cotton, sometimes embroidered with a colorful border. Both men and women wrap themselves in a *shamma* (shawl) for decoration and to keep warm. Most women also wear bright scarves or turbans on their heads.

Three Major World Religions in Ethiopia

Long ago, most people in Ethiopia believed in super-natural beings that lived in certain trees and around water and other places. Some tribes in Ethiopia still organize their lives around their beliefs in spirits. Many Christians, Muslims, and Jews in Ethiopia today believe that certain kinds of sickness are caused by spirits, or that certain people have supernatural power to destroy people or property.

Sometime during the Aksumite empire, Judaism came to Ethiopia. Black Jews, or *Falashas*, lived in near-isolation for many years around Gondar. For hundreds of years with no contact with other Jews, they practiced a simple form of Judaism based on the first five books of the Bible. In 1984 and 1985, Operation Moses and Operation Joshua airlifted more than 8,000 Ethiopian Jews from Sudanese refugee camps to Israel. For years, only a trickle of the remaining Falashas managed to leave the country. Then, over one weekend in the spring of 1991, the Ethiopian government allowed Israeli forces to airlift more than 14,000 Jews to Israel.

Ethiopia is also one of the oldest Christian countries, and about 40 percent of the Ethiopian people are Christian. It is mentioned several times in the Bible and ancient writers called it the land of God. Christianity became the state religion of the Aksumite Kingdom in the early fourth century, then expanded beyond Aksum throughout the highlands.

Originally, the Ethiopian church had close ties to the Syrian Christian church and was then linked with the Egyptian Christian church. But as Egypt became rapidly Muslim after A.D. 642, the Ethiopian Orthodox church became a separate body. Isolated from any Western

An Ethiopian Orthodox church.

Christian influence until the sixteenth century, it developed its own traditions based on strong Old Testament patterns of worship. Today, each church has a holy of holies, an inner court and outer court, and an Ark of the Covenant—just like the ancient Hebrew temple. People remove their shoes before entering many churches and women are not allowed in some. The Orthodox Church also has a rich heritage of chanting, singing, and dancing.

Until the communist revolution in 1974, Christianity was the official religion of Ethiopia and greatly shaped Ethiopian culture. After the revolution, government leaders closed down foreign mission stations, looted churches, and jailed hundreds of Ethiopian church leaders. Later, the government relaxed its anti-church pressure. Many new churches were built. Now more people than ever go to church or worship in house churches.

Impact of Islam

Islam, the second major religion in Ethiopia, also came to Ethiopia during the time of the Aksumite Kingdom. Perhaps 45 percent of the country's people are Muslims. The ancient walled city of Harar is the center of Islamic culture in Ethiopia. Although some people considered the war in the north to be a religious conflict, Eritrea's two million people are divided almost evenly between Christianity and Islam.

Along with everything else, religion is changing in Ethiopia. Many rich priests fled or were killed when the communists took over in 1974. In the northern part of the country, where the church used to collect huge land taxes, priests plow and sow like other farmers, mixing their teaching and religious skills with peasant life. Long-time divisions are breaking down in places. The alternative government in Tigre gave political representation and land to Muslims, who could traditionally only live by trade or crafts. Until recently in Eritrea, Muslims and Christians would not eat food prepared by people of other faiths. Now, Muslim-Christian marriages are common.

Eyes and Crosses

Ethiopian art began in the church. Artists drew scenes from the Bible on wood or parchment made from animal skins or on church buildings. Important people or important parts of the story were drawn larger to emphasize their importance. Good people were usually shown with both eyes looking straight ahead, while bad people were shown looking to the side, with only one eye showing. Most of this early art was not designed to look real but to tell the story as clearly as possible.

Artists used bold, bright colors, especially red, yellow, blue, and green, and often filled their paintings with geometric patterns. People stare out of the paintings with large, expressive eyes. Eyes border some churches and doorways. Artists also drew crosses, still important to Ethiopian art, and many saints, especially St. George, Ethiopia's favorite saint.

An example of traditional art can be seen on the cover of Paul Simon's Grammy-winning album, *Graceland*, which uses an Ethiopian painting of St. George killing the dragon. A more modern dragon, representing colonialism, can be seen in one of the well-known stained glass windows in Africa Hall in Addis Ababa.

The church used to be the main patron of artists, but after the revolution, art was sponsored by the government as well. During a National Cultural and Economic

Development Campaign, every town and kebele was encouraged to set up its own *kinet guad* (cultural troupe) of singers, dancers, poets, and writers. Each kinet guad explored the dances, music, and culture of its own area. A professional national troupe put on shows with pieces from all of the different areas.

Art of the Countryside

Most crafts in Ethiopia are done as part of daily work. But some jewelers, blacksmiths, weavers, and potters make their living with little home craft industries.

For many years, these craftspeople were even poorer than most Ethiopians, and they were not respected. Sometimes they were insulted or blamed for village sicknesses. Blacksmiths, who were especially looked down on, were believed to practice magic, and turn themselves into hyenas at night. In the early twentieth century, Emperor Menelik worked hard to eradicate the superstition against iron workers because he believed Ethiopia's future needs, both for farming tools and weapons, depended on them. The government still tries to wipe out old prejudices against craftspeople.

Baskets are made in every region of Ethiopia from natural plant fibers, and are sometimes dyed bright colors. The city of Harar is famous for the brightest baskets and colorful markets. Weavers know how to waterproof

some baskets, which are then used to hold food and water. In most Ethiopian homes, the *mesob* (table) is a large kind of basket.

Although wood is scarce, carvers southwest of Addis Ababa make three-legged stools from single pieces of sycamore wood. Men on the plains who wear a fancy hairdo shaped with clay make a tiny stool to prop under their necks while they sleep so as not to ruin their hairdos.

Ethiopians are known for beautiful jewelry. Traditionally, a woman's riches were her jewelry, and almost all women in Ethiopia still wear jewelry of some kind. Silver and almost pure gold from the countryside are made into delicate crosses of all shapes and sizes. Crosses have been made near Lalibela since the tenth century and Gondar since the seventeenth and eighteenth centuries.

Red clay is used to create simple, graceful jars, dishes, and bowls, made without potter's wheels. Depending on how the piece is fired, it might end up red, gray, or shiny black. Women make pots for cooking, carrying water, and storing things. Coffee pots, with either one or two spouts, are made for brewing and pouring coffee, an important drink in every home.

Recently, craftspeople have begun to turn sheep and goat wool (always used for clothes and caps by people in the highest, coldest parts of the country) into fine rugs and woolen clothes. But cotton, native to Ethiopia, is more common. Ethiopia now has cotton factories, but women

Ethiopian craftspeople are famous for weaving beautiful baskets out of dried grasses.

Many of the musical instruments used in traditional Ethiopian music are made out of wood.

in the countryside still spin, and men weave on wooden looms out in the open air. Even on power looms, clothes are often made with traditional designs.

Folk Songs, Church Songs, War Songs

Musical instruments, made from wood, bamboo, animal skins, pottery, or metal, are sometimes fancy and always shaped with care. From the simple gourd or whistle of a shepherd boy to the dignified *bagana* (a large wooden harp like the biblical David's harp), musical instruments are treasured. The *masenqo* (a one-stringed fiddle) and the *washint* (a four-holed flute that sounds something like a recorder) are the most popular instruments, used for folk but not church music. Most highland villages have at least one masenqo player. Drums are also heard everywhere, in churches, at dances, sometimes all night before weddings. A *sistrum* (metal rattle), shaken back and forth, helps keep the rhythm.

Church chants are an important part of Ethiopian music, and the entire Orthodox church service, except for the scripture readings, is sung. According to the old stories, every chant used by the Orthodox church was created by Saint Yared, "the father of Ethiopian music." The legend says he had trouble learning when he was a young monk, but was inspired by a caterpillar trying to climb a tree. After falling again and again, the caterpillar finally succeeded. Yared went back to his studies, and he succeeded so well that he wrote all the chants used today.

One famous painting shows Saint Yared playing for a king. The king's spear had slipped and pierced Saint Yared's foot, but Saint Yared plays on. Both men are so caught up in the music that neither one notices the spear.

Debteras are special church musicians who carry on Saint Yared's legacy. They may spend up to twenty years studying church songs, dance, poetry, literature, and theology.

Lalibalotch and *azmaris* are other types of Ethiopian musicians. Many lalibalotch have leprosy, a disease of the skin. Forbidden to mix with other people, they slip out of hiding in the hour before sunrise, and are the shadowy figures who sing melancholy songs and receive money or food in the gateways of the rich. Azmaris, or minstrels, with their ballads and verses, are like the jesters in the medieval courts of Europe. Through the hidden humor of their songs, they poke fun at the high and mighty.

But Ethiopian music is not left to trained musicians. Almost everyone in Ethiopia dances and sings. When the music calls, people participate by clapping, chanting, or singing along with the chorus or joining in the dance. Music is part of joyful and sad and ordinary occasions. Until very recently, the ancient simple rhythms of Ethiopian folk music were not diluted by outside influences.

Zanfan is an Amharic word used both for folk songs and dances, because the two are hardly ever separate. A chorus of men and women sing and clap, and women break in with shrill cries of "ley, ley, ley" to spur on soloists who often make up the verses to work songs, love songs, songs of lullaby and war as they go along. As with most Ethiopian music, the rhythms are simple, but the words are not. Men going home from work will suddenly make up an elaborate zanfan with humorous comments on everything that happened to them during the day. A winning team will rush off the field making up a song that mentions every member of the team, their coach, their school, and their opponents. Zanfan dances are also made up on the spot, with much shaking of the shoulders but not fancy footwork.

Eskista, a kind of dance performed by very fast rhythmic movements of the neck and shoulders, is common to most highland people. At moments of excitement, the dancers suck air sharply through their teeth, making a sound like "eskista." Other ethnic groups also have their own folk dances and songs. The Dorze have an acrobatic dance with somersaults and cartwheels. The Guraghe use graceful footwork in their dances. One Oromo dance uses mostly the head. In another Oromo dance, a woman dancer puts her arms over the shoulders of two other women and then stamps her feet very hard, making a sharp "tss-tss-tss" sound through clenched teeth.

The Gojjam are known for songs of love and athletic dances. A man leaps into the air wriggling his shoulders and neck, and other men follow, each trying to leap higher than the other. Wollamo songs and dances are famous for their rhythm. The Afar wear bright clothes and the chief waves a dagger, while the men dance with wooden lances and the women with bright umbrellas.

When Ethiopians feel they cannot speak out against injustice or intolerance, when they want to celebrate, or when they want to mourn, music gives them a voice to say what they want to say.

3. The Longest Human History in the World

Ethiopia has a story quite different from that of any other African country. Throughout the nineteenth century, while Africa was being colonized, only Ethiopia was able to remain independent. It was also the only country in Africa to develop its own form of writing. More recently, Ethiopia fought the longest war on the African continent. Each of these facts has roots in Ethiopian history, a history that goes back a long time.

Lucy

In 1974, Dr. Donald Johanson was exploring in the Afar Triangle, an isolated part of the Great Rift Valley two hundred miles northeast of Addis Ababa. On the afternoon of November 30, he looked down and saw the fossil of an elbow joint on the ground. As he knelt and brushed away the dry soil, he uncovered the back of a skull. He had discovered the bones of the most complete and oldest hominid skeleton ever found. Because his research team was listening to the Beatles song "Lucy in the Sky with Diamonds" on the day they found the skeleton, they named it Lucy.

Lucy, who has been dated between 2.9 million and

Some of the oldest human fossils have been found in Ethiopia's Great Rift Valley.

3.6 million years old, appears to be one of our oldest relatives. Johanson believes that Lucy is part of a never-before discovered species, *Australopithecus afarensis,* the oldest known ancestor of human beings. Other scientists believe that she may be an unusual member of an already discovered species, *Australopithecus africanus*—which also may have evolved into the *homo* line. Either way, Ethiopia may well be the birthplace of humankind.

As humans changed over thousands of years, our ancestors left behind tools and art as well as their remains. In Ethiopia, scientists have discovered large stone hand axes, sharp instruments made from volcanic glass called obsidian, and drawings on limestone caves near Dire Dawa that show people hunting and herding cattle.

Archaeological evidence shows that by 5000 B.C., small groups of hunters and gatherers roamed the Ethiopian plateau. In the northwest plateau highlands, they began to grow plants, including wheat and barley and *tef*, a tiny grain. Sometime before 2000 B.C., they were sowing and plowing fields of grains, and raising animals for food instead of relying on hunting.

The Ancient Aksumite Kingdom

Meanwhile, by around 1000 B.C., a kingdom called Saba (Sheba) had developed across the Red Sea on the southwest tip of Arabia. The Sabaeans had a complicated society. They farmed using irrigation and terraces, made fine jewelry and coins, and traded with other people along the coast of Africa and as far away as India. They were Semites—people who spoke Semitic languages like Arabic or Hebrew. Sometime after 1000 B.C., they moved across the Red Sea and up onto the Ethiopian plateau where they began to intermarry with the Ethiopian people. Out of these people grew the mighty Aksum civilization.

The Aksumites built stone palaces, temples, and obelisks (tall, decorated pillars usually raised over the graves of important people). They produced coins of gold, silver, and copper to use in trade with Arabia, Egypt, and India. At first, the Aksumite Kingdom was just a capital city and a small amount of surrounding land. Gradually, it expanded over all of northern and some of central Ethiopia. Geez, the earliest written language of Ethiopia, became the main language of the area.

Five languages spoken in Ethiopia today come from Geez, the "Latin of Ethiopia," which is still used in church services and church poetry. Amharic, which probably evolved during the Middle Ages, is written with the same letters as Geez but with additional letters for new sounds like *j*, *sh*, *ch*, and *gw*.

One God

New religions also came to Ethiopia during the Aksumite empire. All Semitic cultures embraced the idea of one god. The three great western religions—Judaism, Christianity, and Islam—originated among Semitic peoples.

According to Ethiopian tradition, the Queen of Sheba (Saba), mentioned in the Bible, traveled from Aksum to King Solomon's Israelite kingdom in the mid-900s B.C. If this legend is true, Jewish beliefs and practices entered Ethiopia at that time. A small group of Ethiopian Jews, the Falasha, claim to be descended from the sons of Israelite leaders who came to Ethiopia with Sheba's son. Other people think Judaism spread from southern Arabia.

However it came, we know it is very ancient because the Falasha use only the Torah (the first five books of the Bible) and do not include any later Jewish customs or festivals.

During the fourth, fifth, and sixth centuries, small bands of Syrian missionaries introduced Christianity to the Aksumite empire. During the reign of King Ezana, coins began to be stamped with the cross of Christ. King Ezana started the first Christian churches in Ethiopia around 330 to 335 A.D. and Christianity became the state religion of Aksum.

Islam came to Ethiopia when a group of persecuted Muslims fled to Aksum around A.D. 615 because their leader, the prophet Mohammed, had described Ethiopia as "a land of righteousness where no one was wronged." The ruler of Arabia, who had not yet accepted Islam, sent messengers asking that the Muslims be turned over to him. But the emperor of Aksum said no, not even for a mountain of gold. In thanks, Mohammed ordered his followers not to bother Ethiopia.

During the seventh century, Muslims swept over most countries of the area in a *jihad*, or Holy War, forcing people to accept the religion of Islam. Ethiopia was soon surrounded by Islamic countries and many tribes in what is now Ethiopia adopted the new religion. But the central highlands of Ethiopia, thanks to the ancient kindness of the Aksumite emperor, escaped the jihad.

No one is sure why the Aksumite Kingdom ended. Fighting along the Red Sea during the jihad seems to have blocked trade. The Beja people from the north invaded Aksum and pushed the Aksumites south into Agew lands. Eventually the Agew people resisted. Ethiopian tradition says that a tenth-century Agew Falasha princess called Yudit (Judith) and her army galloped against Aksum's rulers and destroyed the city of Aksum and hundreds of churches. The empire fell. But the Amhara and Tigre people today consider Aksum to be an important part of their heritage.

Struggles of the Amhara

For about 150 years, the Zagwe rulers of the Agew people disrupted the line of kings claiming to be descended from King Solomon and the Queen of Sheba. But the Zagwe kings did stay true to Christianity. King Lalibela, the most famous, was disturbed by the Islamic conquest of Jerusalem and vowed to build a new Jerusalem in Ethiopia. He had twelve churches carved out of solid rock. Legends say that the workers were helped by angels who did twice as much work at night as the people did during the day.

While the Agew were in control, the Amhara-Tigre culture went into a time of isolation called its dark ages. Then in about 1270, the Amhara people revolted against the Zagwe kings. The new king, Yekumo Amlak, claimed he had a right to rule because he was descended from King Solomon and the Queen of Sheba.

One of the greatest periods of Ethiopian history began, a time of great literature and art and music. For the next 250 years, the Amhara homeland of Shoa was the center of political power, and both the Amharic language and Orthodox Christianity spread over most of what is now central Ethiopia. In the east, the Amhara kings recaptured lands that had become Muslim so that, for the first time, Ethiopian kings now ruled over large Muslim populations from their mobile tent cities.

Elsewhere, the Turks had become the world's greatest military power, sweeping over Africa and the Middle East in a jihad that brought the Islamic faith to the eastern edge of Europe. In the eleventh, twelfth, and thirteenth centuries, European noblemen, knights, and commoners set out on at least nine great crusades to recapture or defend the holy land (birthplace of Christianity) from the Turks. For three centuries, Christian European rulers sent explorers to find a legendary Christian king, named Prester John, to aid them in their fight against the Muslims.

The real Prester John may in fact have been one of the Christian emperors of Ethiopia. Fantastic stories about this priest-king, and a search for his kingdom, continued until the sixteenth century. But Ethiopia could hardly help defend Jerusalem because the Muslims eventually threatened her borders, too.

In 1527, Muslims attacked from the east and established a capital at Harar. A fierce leader named Ahmad Gran (the Left Handed) led his armies across almost the whole Ethiopian plateau. They destroyed churches, burned books and pictures, and carried off treasure. In 1540, Portugal, one of the few countries successful in stopping Turkish expansion, sent help to the struggling Ethiopian kingdom. With Portuguese guns, the Amhara were eventually able to end the Muslim invasion, stop Agew revolts, and bring the people of the eastern lowlands under control. But the fighting left the country poorer, with many cattle killed and people carried off by the Muslims to be slaves in Arab lands.

While the Muslims were attacking from the east, the Oromo began to move up from the south. Throughout the 1700s, they attacked, raided, and sometimes settled across the Ethiopian plateau. Within thirty years, they had spread into about one-third of the country. But though they were fierce warriors, they did not try to form an Oromo nation or force their religion and culture on people as the Amhara and Muslims did. Eventually, about twelve Oromo groups developed, each different—in religious beliefs, way of life, and even language—from the others.

In 1636, Emperor Fasiladas, with Portuguese help, had built a new capital, Gondar. For more than two centuries, Amhara kings built fine castles and churches in

Gondar. But having a stable capital, instead of tent cities that could move whenever a king sensed trouble, may have led to a loss of power for the Amhara kings. In any case, in the last part of the eighteenth century, rulers of different Ethiopian provinces became more independent and began to fight with each other.

Zamena Mesafint

This period, nearly a century long, was called the *zamena mesafint*. Slave trade was often the only contact with other countries. In the zamena mesafint, each province had its own king, and people felt loyalty to their own province, not to a country called Ethiopia.

Amhara kings commanded enormous respect, power, and land. Their subjects, who were not allowed to even look at them, had to bow and kiss the king's feet. Oromo kings, on the other hand, did not own all the land in their territories, and their subjects did not bow. Some Oromo, however, did borrow ideas of kingship from neighboring Amhara provinces. One Oromo king, Abba Jifar II, insisted on being carried everywhere by two servants, one supporting each arm, so that his feet never touched the ground.

The Beginnings of Modern Ethiopia

Starting in 1855, four strong emperors brought back

central rule, expanded the empire, and shaped modern Ethiopia. The first, Theodore II, was a remarkable man. He was not from the royal line but he was a strong warrior. He reorganized the army, and by using cannons and roads, brought many of the provinces under his rule. Although he had big dreams, he was opposed by many who did not see the need for unity, and was not able to fulfill his dreams in his lifetime. Over a quarrel with the British government, Theodore shot himself on April 13, 1868, rather than be captured by British soldiers.

The next two emperors, Yohannes and Menelik II, tripled the territory under central control, adding dozens of tribes and millions of people to Ethiopia. Emperor Yohannes, who ruled from 1871 to 1889, came from Tigre. As emperor, he struggled against several foreign invasions—Egyptian armies in 1875 and 1876 and Italian armies in 1887. While resisting invaders from Sudan, Yohannes was killed by a sniper's bullet.

Menelik II, an Amhara, had been imprisoned by Emperor Theodore when he was only eleven, but he was inspired by Theodore's dream. After he escaped from prison, he reorganized the government of the Shoa region and spread his power, taking control of Tigre and areas to the south and southeast. Eventually, he united all the provinces, including some that had been cut off for centuries. In 1889, he was crowned emperor of all Ethiopia.

The biggest threat to his rule came when the Italian

A statue of King Menelik, who was crowned emperor of Ethiopia in 1889 after uniting the various tribal groups.

government, which had started a colony in Eritrea, began to push into Ethiopian land. In 1896, Emperor Menelik II fought Italian armies at Aduwa, the capital of Tigre Province, and won a decisive victory.

The battle at Aduwa stopped Italian expansion. But two things happened that are part of Ethiopia's modern struggle. First, Eritrea stayed under Italian rule. Second, Menelik's army of about eighty thousand people had to live off the land as it went north through Tigre and other provinces. More Tigreans than Italians died defending their homes against Menelik's army.

Menelik's rule brought schools, banks, roads, the first telegraph machine, and the first motor car in 1907 to Ethiopia. The emperor loved to try new things. It was said of him: "If a builder of castles in the air came to Ethiopia with a plan to construct an escalator from the earth to the moon, Menelik would have asked him to build it, if only to see whether it could be done."

Menelik's first capital was at the top of a mountain, safe from attack. However, it was also cold and wet and far away from food and wood, so he moved it to the nearby plain in 1887. His wife, Taitu, pleased with her new home, named it *Addis Ababa* (new flower). But Tigre people were not pleased with this decision to move the center of power farther south.

When Menelik died in 1913, the country plunged into crisis. After fighting within the royal family, Menelik's daughter Zauditu was made empress in 1916, while Ras Tafari, the son of Menelik's cousin, was named regent and heir to the throne. When Empress Zauditu died in 1930, Ras Tafari was crowned Emperor Haile Selassie I, *negusa negast* (king of kings).

King of Kings

In his forty-four-year reign, Haile Selassie tried to make life better for his poor and powerless subjects. In 1931, he provided the first written constitution, which provided for an elected parliament. But without roads and a good communication system for the rural countryside, few people were ever able to vote. And poor rural people, of course, were never elected to the government.

The emperor was committed to development and social change. While he was still regent, he established the first printing press, built hospitals, and founded schools in Ethiopia. As king, he abolished slavery, set up the first state bank, and brought in a radio station and foreign experts to train his army.

His string of successes ended in 1934 when Mussolini, the ruler of Italy, declared he would revenge Italian defeat at Aduwa and settle large numbers of people in Ethiopia. Using the most modern weapons available, he attacked. Haile Selassie I went into exile. In a famous statement before the League of Nations, the emperor asked for help in fighting the Italians, but no country responded. The Italian army killed many Ethiopians, including Abuna Petros, head of the Orthodox church, and set up a segregated society. Ethiopian patriots, though, never stopped fighting for their freedom.

When World War II started and Mussolini declared war on Britain and France, British soldiers came to the aid of Ethiopian soldiers. Haile Selassie returned to Ethiopia in 1941 and led the Ethiopian forces to liberation against the Italian armies.

Return of Haile Selassie

When the war was over, the emperor redoubled his efforts to reconstruct and modernize the country and to encourage basic education, which was desperately needed since the Italians had executed almost everyone who could read or who had professional skills.

Haile Selassie also made religious changes. In 1948, the Orthodox church cut its last strings with Egypt, and the emperor gained the power to appoint bishops. The boundaries between church and state became blurred, although the 1955 constitution recognized the right of all religions to exist without interference. Haile Selassie often spoke out for religious tolerance. In his efforts to unify the country, he not only married an Oromo woman but often met with Muslim leaders.

The emperor's drive to unify the country led him to

establish a national airline in 1946. Using old U.S. Dakotas left over from World War II, Ethiopian Airlines opened up the back country and improved communications. The first wheels many rural Ethiopians have seen, even today, are underneath an EAL airplane.

Despite these efforts to make Ethiopia a strong, centralized nation, ethnic loyalties still ran strong. After Haile Selassie's return, Tigre peasants asserted their independence and sought to avenge grievances that went back to Menelik's reign. They revolted against the central government. The emperor quickly crushed the revolt, declared Amharic the official language, and confiscated large areas of good land in the south and west of Tigre.

Under this system, Tigre peasants became tenant farmers who could not build up any reserves for drought years and had to work very hard to scrape out a living. Over-farming eroded the land and depleted the soil.

At the same time, trouble was brewing in Eritrea. After World War II, the United Nations had federated Eritrea with Ethiopia but had allowed it to keep control of its own domestic affairs. But the emperor feared that a separate Eritrea would encourage other ethnic groups to form their own separatist movements and he dissolved the Eritrean parliament in 1962. Eritrea was annexed as a regular province. These policies planted the seeds of war and famine that still threaten to destroy northern Ethiopia.

End of the Time of Kings

During the 1970s, life became even harder for Ethiopia's poor. In 1972 and 1973, parts of the country got only scattered showers of rain. By November 1973, nearly 1.6 million people were suffering from drought and famine. Crowds of peasants, begging for food, lined the highway between Addis Ababa and Asmara. The Ethiopian government, however, ignored the famine until international broadcasts began to put pressure on the high levels of government.

In the end, Haile Selassie failed his people. By 1974, Ethiopia was probably the poorest country in Africa and one of the poorest in the world. Haile Selassie's policies on land, Eritrea, drought, and inflation, compounded by his old age, brought the time of kings in Ethiopia to an end.

Transportation workers and teachers and students began to demonstrate against the government and call for change. Other groups followed, but only the army was organized enough to actually overthrow Haile Selassie. A military committee called the Derg took over most of the government in the summer of 1974. They put out a policy statement called *Ethiopia Tikdem*, or Ethiopia First, and began to arrest members of Haile Selassie's court. On September 12, the Derg arrested Haile Selassie himself. The emperor left his palace with dignity, and rode in the back of a small Volkswagen to prison in the basement of Menelik's old palace.

At first, it looked as if peaceful solutions might be found for many of Ethiopia's old problems. The new head of state, General Aman Andom, who was Eritrean, visited many Eritrean villages to listen and explore possible solutions to the war. The Derg sent students and teachers out into the countryside to draw rural people into the national changes and teach basic living skills. But this notion of peaceful change was soon shattered by a power struggle within the Derg. In one "Saturday night massacre," Aman was killed and about sixty other high-ranking members of the old government were executed.

Red Terror

Ethiopia was then plunged into a year of kye shiber (red terror). Colonel Mengistu Haile Mariam, the new head of state, set up a Marxist-Leninist government and called for all enemies of the government to be executed. Five hundred students were rounded up and killed in May 1977. Each morning, people in Addis Ababa woke up to find bodies on the sidewalks and streets. In the countryside, the government began an unpopular campaign to collectivize farming. Six hundred thousand northern peasants were forced from their farms, and eight million unwilling farmers were placed on collective state farms.

Ironically, Mengistu's government was eventually criticized for the same faults as the government it replaced. In 1984 and 1985, more than half a million people in Ethiopia starved. Television brought the suffering into living rooms around the world, and millions of dollars were donated to bring food to starving people. But inadequate transportation, government policies, poor farming methods, environmental problems, and war made more starvation certain, even when rains were good— and northern Ethiopia had poor rains in 1987, 1989 and 1990.

Mengistu's regime disrupted more people's lives and took away more human rights than the regime of any Ethiopian emperor ever did. The new government also continued some of the bad patterns of the emperors. It did not give minority ethnic groups an adequate voice in decisions. Civil war and border disputes led to huge military expenses.

Droughts in 1990 and 1991, the worst since the famine of 1984 and 1985, were made worse by intense fighting at the Eritrean port of Massawa, where much of the food donated by other countries is shipped. More than fifteen years after the revolution, Ethiopian people are at least as poor and close to disaster as they were before 1974.

Yet some good changes also happened. Mengistu's government attempted to distribute land more fairly and increase opportunities for education. Health managers were put through a two-year training and then sent into rural communities. A network of all-weather roads was built. With foreign help, some parts of the country moved away from famine—trying new grains, finding safe water supplies, building bridges and roads.

Change for the Better

Besides its internal problems, Ethiopia has also had to deal with increasing tensions among all East African countries. Ethiopia periodically accuses the Sudan of allowing various Ethiopian liberation groups to operate from Sudanese borders, and Sudan blames Ethiopia for the same thing. In 1977, when neighboring Somalia went to war with Ethiopia over a southeast region called the Ogaden, the Ethiopian government asked the Soviet Union for help. For about ten years, the Soviet Union provided money and weapons to Ethiopia, while Cuba provided thousands of troops.

In the late 1980s, Mengistu's regime began to make some changes. The Soviet Union, faced with its own economic problems, stopped providing money for Ethiopia's government. Cuban troops left. Signs and banners of Marx and Lenin came down around Addis Ababa. With his government nearly out of money, Mengistu announced on March 5, 1990, the end of the

A monument to Socialism rises above the rooftops in Addis Ababa.

Soviet-style economic system.

Despite these changes and despite pressure from the Soviet Union and the U.S., the Eritrean civil war continued. In February 1991, a loose coalition of rebel groups called the Ethiopian People's Revolutionary Democratic Front (EPRDF) began to attack government troops—with great success. In many places, discouraged government soldiers fled, leaving their weapons behind. Using these captured weapons, the EPRDF marched to within 75 miles of Addis Ababa. On May 21, President Mengistu resigned and left the country. One week later, rebel troops seized the capital.

At negotiation talks in London, the EPRDF agreed to set up a provisional government that would include all major ethnic groups in Ethiopia. Its leaders promised to work toward democratic elections in about a year. Meanwhile, the Eritrean Liberation Front also set up a provisional government in Eritrea, stating they would ask the United Nations to vote on whether Eritrea should be independent from Ethiopia.

Many Ethiopians at home and abroad feel more optimistic that their country can now live in peace. They are waiting to see what will happen next.

4. Stories of Snakes and Kings

Ethiopian legend says that when God was making the world, he decided to make people out of clay. The first batch of people burned. God threw them down to earth where they landed on the continent of Africa and became the African tribes. The second batch was underbaked. They were too white. God threw them down where they became the people of Europe. Finally, God baked a perfect batch. He put these light brown people at the top of the world in Ethiopia where they would be close to his heart.

Since the Aksumite Kingdom, Ethiopian stories have celebrated the glories of Ethiopia. The ancient Tigreans saw themselves as a superior people, though they also admired the culture of the Jewish and Arabian people who had invaded their country for centuries. The tales of Aksum talked not only about how good the land of Judah was, but how much better the land of Ethiopia was.

In the early 1300s, Tigrean priests wrote down many of the traditional stories and gathered them into a book, *Kibre Negest* (*Glory of Kings*). *Kibre Negest*, often called the most important work of Ethiopian literature, became popular with Amhara and Tigrean people and stayed popular for a long time.

Night Visit to a Queen

At the heart of *Kibre Negest* is the story of King Solomon and the Queen of Sheba. As the story begins, a horrible serpent was ravaging the land and killing hundreds of animals every day. The people declared that anyone who could kill the serpent would be their king. A wise man made poison *injera* (bread) and fed it to a goat. When the serpent ate the goat, it fell dead and the man became king.

When the king died, his daughter, Makeda, became his successor, but the people refused to be ruled by a woman. Makeda brought the serpent back to life again. Soon the people begged Makeda to be queen. She was crowned Queen of Sheba.

During the reign of Sheba, a wise Aksumite merchant named Tamrin traveled to the court of Israel's mighty King Solomon. Impressed by the king's intellect, Tamrin returned to Ethiopia to tell Sheba about wise Solomon. The queen wanted to see this great ruler, so she traveled to the land of Israel to King Solomon's court. While she was there, she gave up worshiping the sun and embraced the God of Israel.

Finally she made ready to return to her own land. But Solomon, who was impressed by her great wealth and beauty, invited her to dine with him on the last evening. Over dinner, he suggested a contest: If she took anything of his without permission, she would agree to spend the night with him. Sheba agreed. She drifted to sleep, confident that she could win the contest. Late that night, she suddenly woke in terrible thirst from the spicy meal. She sat up and groped for the glass of water beside her bed. As she drank, Solomon stepped out from the shadows and reminded her of her promise.

Back in her own land, the queen bore a son to Solomon. When he was old enough, he went off to live at his father's court where he learned the ancient Israelite customs and stories. When he was ready to leave his father's land, he prepared to take the firstborn sons of many important Israelite people, but the young men refused to move away from the Ark of the Covenant, the special box that held the laws of Moses. In the dark of the night, they switched pieces of wood for the ark, and hurried away with the real ark. Solomon and his army thundered after. Hearing the noise, Solomon's son and his companions knew they were doomed. But just before the army reached the young men, they were lifted above the ground and across the Red Sea to safety in Ethiopia, where Solomon's son was crowned emperor, Menelik I.

The early parts of *Kibre Negest* emphasized the glory of Israel's royal line. The union of Sheba and Solomon then implied that the glory passed from the Israelites to the Ethiopian kings who were in power at the time *Kibre Negest* was written. Some people, in fact, argue that the only reason it was written was to show that the Amhara line of kings had a right to seize power. It seems, however, that at least the main stories of *Kibre Negest* were told and passed down from parents to children long before the Amhara kings took over. In any case, *Kibre Negest* became a powerful national myth that helped transform Ethiopia from a collection of separate kingdoms into one country.

Magnificent Prester John, the Priest-King

For many years, people outside Ethiopia made up legends about the mysterious land they could not easily explore. During the Middle Ages, Europeans were very interested in Ethiopia, which they considered to be the only Christian country outside of Europe.

In 1165, European rulers received a letter supposedly written by a fantastic priest-king called Prester John. According to the legends, Prester John ruled from an enchanted palace of gold and jewels. With a magic mirror, he could see all of his lands at one glance. He was waited on by dukes and kings as he sat at magic tables made of emerald and amethyst, wearing robes woven by salamanders and washed in fire. Pope Alexander III wrote back to Prester John asking him to send messengers to Rome, and explorers were encouraged to go east to find this mighty king and ask his help in fighting the Crusades.

But people were just as ready to imagine Ethiopia as

a savage and frightening land. Roman mapmakers decided Ethiopia was a land of terrible monsters. Some maps of Ethiopia from the Middle Ages show monstrous creatures named Himantopodes and Blemmyes and one-eyed Ethiopian kings who ate panthers and lions.

Magic Serpents

Dating back to before the time when Sheba controlled the serpent, Ethiopians believed that serpents had special powers. The Mensa people tell a story of a huge white snake with big eyes that could kill people with a look. Tigreans still believe that serpents guard monasteries in their area. People who live near Mount Bor believe that a giant serpent helped that create the world can make earthquakes when it is angry.

The Serpent Ladder of Debra Damo

About fourteen hundred years ago, Ethiopia had many Christian hermits who looked for places to get away from the noise of the world. One monastery—where monks still live—was built on top of an *amba* (table mountain) with steep, smooth sides. Priests and visitors can reach the top only by climbing a rope and animals are hauled up in baskets. Legend tells that the first person climbed up a magic serpent and hung the rope for others to follow.

A Poetic Way of Talking

Tradition says that Amharic developed as a secret language during the time of Queen Judith, and the Amhara are still fond of witty stories with a double meaning that not just anybody can understand. The Amhara and other Ethiopian groups also like to repeat jokes and wise sayings and tell stories with their songs and dances.

Ethiopians repeat many proverbs and have a saying for almost every occasion. In Amharic, even ordinary speech is very expressive. The word *ayezo*, which we would translate as "cheer up," literally means "don't let it seize you." If a drawer sticks, a person will say, "*Imbialla*" ("It says 'refuse'"). When the rainy season is over, people will say, "*Kerempt tebe*" ("It is milked dry"). The country's long Christian heritage is reflected in the words for thank you (literally, "May God give it to you for me") and in what people say if someone is sick, even with a cold: "*Egziabeher yemari*" ("May God spare you").

After the 1974 revolution, the government declared that the revolution would change the country's customs, jokes, and stories. But jokes and stories are hard to stamp out. Today, as always, Ethiopian people tell jokes and stories about themselves, their country, and their new leaders.

A young boy laughs during a storytelling session. Sharing stories and legends is a favorite pastime in Ethiopia.

5. Thirteen Months of Celebrations

Each Ethiopian month has exactly thirty days. The leftover five or six days are gathered into a short thirteenth month called *Pagame*. Every one of the thirteen months has days for celebration. Though Ethiopians work hard, they also know how to relax. If you are pushing someone to finish a project, he may tell you, *"Ishi, nege"* ("Okay; tomorrow"). This is his way of saying that you should relax and appreciate the moment, not worry so much about forcing the world to behave as you want.

Almost all Ethiopian festivals, as well as weddings, funerals, and other special occasions, are celebrated with feasts and dancing. When a wealthy person gives a feast, he invites not only family and friends but also people who are too poor to ever invite him back. When a wealthy person dies, poor priests and debteras are fed at the banquet, which had led to the saying: "St. George, kill only the rich." Large feasts go on for three days.

Traditionally, drinks at a feast are poured to the top or over the top of the glass. No matter how much a guest eats, a host will say, "You spoiled my feast by not eating a thing. Let me give you more." Or the host will scoop up a huge bite of spicy food to place in the guest's mouth.

For many people, festival days are the only times

when they do not work. Although parents are strict with their daughters, during festivals girls can get away with a little flirting. Men and women, who usually do not dance together, take turns dancing, accompanied by Ethiopian flute, violin, and drums. Sometimes a leader sings a story and the other dancers answer together at the end of each sentence while they clap their hands. In another popular type of song, the *fukura*, a warrior struts up and down and sings of his mighty deeds.

Religious Fasts and Festivals

Before the revolution, over half the country's holidays were religious festivals. When Christianity was Ethiopia's official religion, Christian church holidays were also national holidays. Muslims also celebrated their own religious holidays, such as Ramadan and Mohammed's birthday.

An Orthodox Christian's year is organized around more than two hundred fast days when people generally do not eat before noon and do not eat meat, eggs, cheese, butter, or milk at all—so the many feast days are extra special. For example, the fast before Easter lasts two months. As you can imagine, people are ready to celebrate when Easter comes. In fact, the Amharic word for Easter means "great feast."

Ethiopian Christmas is celebrated on our January 7.

Priests and other devout Christians fast and go to special church services for several days beforehand. On Christmas Eve, services last until after midnight. Then the feast begins. All Christmas Day, people eat and play games. Tradition says that if you don't laugh on Christmas, you will not be happy for the rest of your life.

The word most Ethiopians use for Christmas is *ganna*. Ganna is the name of a game much like field hockey, which is played on Christmas Day mostly by boys and young men. Quiet, respectful boys often become fierce and aggressive while playing ganna, and bones are sometimes broken.

Timket, or Epiphany, our January 19, is a bigger holiday for most Ethiopians than either Christmas or Easter. As Christmas celebrates Christ's birth, Timket celebrates Christ's baptism.

To get ready for Timket, children are given new clothes and every shamma is washed white. On the afternoon before Timket, the village priest begins to beat his drum as a signal that a small box representing the Ark of the Covenant is going to be brought outside. An hour later, the procession begins. The chief priest comes out of the church, followed by another priest carrying the ark wrapped in fancy cloth because people cannot look at the ark. After them come more priests carrying bright umbrellas and huge gold or silver crosses, altar boys in fancy dress, and musicians playing masenqos. Adults

An Ethiopian priest carries the Ark of the Covenant on his head as part of the celebration of Timket.

and children join the procession, which stops often to chant and dance. At nightfall, the procession ends and the ark is put down by a pool. Priests guard the ark all night, dancing and chanting until morning.

Before daybreak, people gather around the pool. Babies are brought to be baptized. Then adults step forward. Priests pour water over people's hands and heads and finally fling water over the crowds to those who cannot reach the pool. Then the debteras form two long lines and begin the stately dance of David to the throb of long drums and the rattle of sistrums. Dances like this have been performed for centuries. Finally, the procession winds its way back to the village. When the ark is safely back in the church, everyone goes home to feast.

Fire and Flowers

Nonchurch holidays throughout the year provide other chances to celebrate. One marks Menelik's victory over the Italian government at the Battle of Aduwa. In February of 1890, Menelik wrote these determined words: "Ethiopia has need of no one; she stretches out her hands to God." Ethiopians celebrate Menelik's victory with feasts and dancing on our March 2.

Buhe, the name of a small holiday, probably comes from the Amhara word for dough, *buho*. Buhe comes in August during a fast time, so since people could not celebrate by feasting, they traditionally had a special ceremony with bread. Because Buhe is a holiday without a feast and it occurs in the middle of the rainy season, adults began to ignore the old ceremony. The holiday was left to children.

In rural towns, boys go from house to house in groups. A boy who knows many Buhe songs leads the singing. The old custom was for people to give bread to the groups. Now they sometimes also give money. The boys then bless the givers with a saying such as:

"If anyone insults the mistress of this house, let him

smell like a bedbug."

The festival ends with a bonfire and with the loud noise of boys cracking homemade whips.

New Year is celebrated on our September 11. The long rainy season has just ended and people cover their floors with fresh cut grass. Children dash around with burning torches they make from the small fires that are everywhere. In traditional white dresses, boys and girls go from house to house in small groups, singing and carrying wild flowers that they give to the mistress of the house. The people in the houses hand out bread, money, or small gifts, much like our Halloween. In cities, where the society is not as strict as in the countryside, a boy will often dance up to a girl and offer her a lemon. If she takes it, they kiss, and become boyfriend and girlfriend.

Maskal, celebrated on our September 27, was once a religious festival based on the legend of the finding of the true cross. According to the story, Queen Helena, mother of the first Christian emperor of Rome, had her subjects set fire to long poles. The smoke bent over and touched the spot where Christ's cross was buried. Although Maskal still celebrates this event, it has also become a festival to welcome the new season.

On Maskal eve, a huge *demera* (pole) is placed up-right in an open space. The next day, women and girls gather yellow maskal daisies to decorate eucalyptus poles, which the men and boys then put around the

Priests chant during a Maskal ceremony.

demera. After a pyramid of poles has been built, the people circle it while the priests chant. In the evening, the bonfire is lit. Young people dance around the flames, shouting, while young men toss lighted torches into the teepee of sticks. Everyone sings special Maskal songs. The next morning, people dip their fingers into the dark ashes from the bonfire and draw the sign of the cross on their foreheads.

These youngsters are taking part in a traditional Ethiopian wedding ceremony.

Weddings and Harvest Festivals

Wedding customs differ from tribe to tribe, but highland weddings all end with a great feast. Often people stay up all night, dancing and singing. In the old days in Eritrea, a bride would come to the wedding and dance until she couldn't dance anymore. Only then could she see the groom. During weddings, people feast for days. In war-torn Eritrea even the unpaid soldiers have a feast. To afford the food and drink, more than a hundred soldiers marry at the same time and split the costs. Weddings between Muslims and Christians used to be very rare, but in the Eritrean army they have become common.

For the people of the plains, wedding customs do not always include a feast, nor—since most people are not Christians—do people celebrate Christmas or Timket. Their festivals are usually built around the seasons and the elements. Men and women have special ceremonies, for example, to bring rain. Farming tribes set aside special days at planting time and later at harvest time. Hunting tribes have their own rituals and celebrations. In one tribe, a shaman used to spit on the spears of the hunters as they went out, to give them good magic.

Ethiopians find chances to celebrate whenever they can. A guest can expect to be served as much food and drink as the household can gather. A man is considered "big" when he is generous in feeding other people. Many Ethiopian proverbs use eating or drinking, such as "Think about what you hear before you speak, chew before you swallow." For the Amhara, the stomach is considered to be the center of wisdom, and a good student is said to have "drunk his lesson."

It may seem strange that many sayings focus around eating in a country where so many people have little to eat. Although many Ethiopian households are very poor, they will still offer their guests a banana or a cup of coffee. Rural people who own little still laugh and dance and celebrate with great enthusiasm.

6. The Bare Necessities of Life

Around daybreak, the animals start to make a commotion in a house of Maji village. Negatwa gets up and opens the door to let the chickens out. One of her six children gets up and leads the cow outside. Negatwa pokes at the burned wood in the center of her dirt floor. Usually, she can find a glowing ember to start up the fire. Today, she can't. So she sends one of the children to a neighbor's house to bring back a burning coal. She covers it with little bits of wood and blows on it until the fire starts again. Then she puts the coffee beans on the fire to roast.

Morning in a Village

One of the first morning jobs is to fetch water. Whenever possible, a village is settled where water is close by. Negatwa gets hers from a spring near the village. Back at the house, she pounds the roasted coffee beans, puts them in a clay pot, and pours water over them. As her children get up, they take turns washing their hands and faces in the cold water. One of the children warms a little water for his father and any guests who are in the house.

For breakfast, the family eats plain *injera*, or bread, left over from the night before, or parched barley, chick

Children perform their morning washing with cold water pulled from a nearby river.

peas, or wheat. Coffee is flavored with salt, sugar, or in some places, a little honey. Children are usually the only ones to drink milk.

After breakfast, everyone has a job. By the time children are three years old, they can help watch the chickens and gather food. When boys and girls are about eight years old, they start doing adult chores. One of Negatwa's older daughters lifts the lid of the iron and puts burning charcoal inside. When the iron is hot, she presses her father's pants.

Negatwa's husband, Wondemu, is the head nurse at the local government clinic. At about 9:00 A.M., he leaves for work. Other men are leaving for the fields. Farmers work hard, long days. In fact the director of the U.S. Office of Foreign Disaster Assistance has called Ethiopian peasants "the most disciplined and hard-working in the world." Old ways change slowly, and in many rural areas the only people who earn respect besides farmers are priests, soldiers, political leaders, lawyers, and medical workers.

Meanwhile, Negatwa's children dress quickly for school. Anyone can go to the government school in Maji, but not all families can afford pencils and notebooks for their children. Many rural families are especially reluctant to send their girls to be educated.

As Negatwa's younger children go off to school, two or three village boys who do not go to school come down the road collecting cows from each household. Boys five years old and older take turns caring for the village cows, sheep, and goats. They take the animals out to pasture and watch them for the day. Negatwa's cow joins the herd.

Negatwa's two oldest daughters have finished the twelfth grade, but they still live at home. There are no husbands for them, since so many young men went to war, and there are no jobs in Maji. They help with household chores, take care of neighborhood children, and help care for Negatwa's parents who live nearby. In many Ethiopian households, aunts, uncles, cousins, and grandparents share a family's house. Older people are respected, to the point that when young boys are asked what they want to be when they grow up, they have been known to answer, "An old man."

After the men and children are gone, the village women gather to have coffee together, and sometimes have something to eat. Then it's time to start the morning chores. Negatwa and her daughters check the bowl of injera dough to see if it's fermenting properly. They might need to add water or flour made of tef, sorghum, wheat, barley, or corn.

A Long Day's Work

Many Ethiopian women are proud of their special recipes, and making meals takes up most of a woman's time. Grain has to be made into flour. Highland women grind their grain with a stone. Lowland women pound grain into flour. Because Negatwa lives in a village, she can send her grain to be ground by machine in town. She then tends the garden with its cabbage, collards, onions, garlic, red peppers, and sometimes corn and squash. Beans grow on the fence. Chickens run around the garden and eat bugs or rest under the shade of the *koba* (false

An Ethiopian woman makes flour for baking by pounding grain until it becomes powdery.

banana plant). *Nug*, a plant similar to a sunflower, is cultivated for oil. Many rural women still tattoo themselves by turning nug oil and soot into a dark blue dye and using an acacia thorn to puncture the skin.

Pounding and mixing spices is an all-day job, and Negatwa does it once a week. On Tuesday or Saturday, she goes to market to buy the spices she needs, along with grain, coarse sugar, meat, lentils, and butter. Then she dries the spices in the sun for several days. When she is satisfied that the spices are ready, she takes a day to pound and mix them.

For women and men all over Ethiopia, it's important to go to market. At the market, they find out what their neighbors are doing, hear any important government pronouncements, trade things, and buy goods from other parts of Ethiopia—salt from the Danakil depression, cotton from the lowlands, crafts from other areas. People bargain to get the best price for what they want to buy.

Near noon, Negatwa starts pouring injera batter on a griddle placed on stones beside the wood fire. Smoke trickles up through the thatch roof, making it sooty. The injera bakes into a thin, sour pancake. She also fixes some boiled corn and a broth with a little meat flavor to dip the injera into. If the children are not coming home to eat lunch, she sends them to school with a stalk of sugar cane. Poorer families might only have grain or a sour bread made from *inset*, the root of the false banana tree.

After lunch, Negatwa and her daughters sweep the dirt floors of their three-room house. Negatwa hangs the blankets over the fence and the bedbugs and fleas hop off in the hot sun. The house does not have much furniture. The family sleeps on beds made from wooden poles and leather straps with a mattress stuffed with tef straw or moss. Younger children sleep on the floor.

In the afternoon, Negatwa and her daughters also need to start baking injera for the evening meal. If you want to see what it's like to work all day fixing food, try this recipe for a vegetable stew.

Alicha (vegetable stew)

1/2 cup oil
1 1/2 cups red onion, finely chopped
6 medium potatoes
5 medium carrots
1 small can tomato paste
1 small cabbage
1 green pepper
6 medium chiles (Anaheim)
1/4 tsp. garlic powder
1/4 tsp. turmeric
1/4 tsp. ground ginger
1/4 tsp. black pepper
salt to taste

☛Peel and slice the carrots. ☛Wash the cabbage and cut it into big pieces. ☛Saute the onions in the oil over low heat. Stir them constantly and don't let them brown. ☛Add tomato paste and mix well. ☛Add the carrots and cabbage. Stir gently and cook until the vegetables are tender. Set this mixture aside. ☛Peel and cut the potatoes. ☛Add them to the mixture. ☛Add the garlic powder, turmeric, and ginger and let the whole thing cook over low heat for 30-45 minutes. ☛Add a little salt and black pepper. ☛Just before serving, slice the green peppers lengthwise and serve them over the stew.

You can also try some Ethiopian food without spending all day in the kitchen. Remember, many Ethiopian women have to start by grinding their own flour, but you can start with a store-bought bag.

Dabo colo (a snack)

1 pie crust mix
water
chile powder or cayenne pepper

☛Mix the pie crust with the water, using the instructions on the box. ☛Add a few shakes of chile powder to the dough, or (if you like spicy food) add 1 teaspoon of cayenne pepper. ☛With your hands, roll the dough into long thin strips. ☛Use a pair of scissors to cut the dough into 1/4" pieces. ☛Cook the pieces on a greased cookie sheet for 8-10 minutes at 450 °.

Daily Afternoon and Evening Routines

Once or twice a week, Negatwa and her daughters carry clothes to the stream for washing. Instead of soap, they use berries from a nearby plant called *endod* and pound the dirt out with their feet. At lunch or after school, the children are sent to gather wood.

Around 4:00 P.M., Wondemu comes home. He gathers with the other village men either at the *tej bet* (local drink house) or at one of the men's houses where they dip cool beer from a log container and sit and talk before the evening meal. Ethiopians make their own beer from barley, corn, or some other grain, plus a plant like hops.

As the sun reaches the horizon, the family starts a flurry of activity. The cows come home and need to be milked. The children bring the cows, chickens, and other animals inside. Everyone does evening chores as dinner is prepared. Just as darkness falls, the family gathers around the mesob for the evening meal. At supper, the biggest meal, they will have a *wat*, a stew made with pepper, spices, butter, oil, seeds, legumes, onions, and sometimes meat.

Several rounds of injera are stacked in a basket and the wat is poured over them. People scoop up bites of wat with pieces of injera.

Afterward, Negatwa's family relaxes around the fire for a little while with the light of beeswax candles

flickering on their faces. Before long, everyone goes to
bed. The animals settle down in a back room. Some of the
children sleep on the floor on animal skins. The others
crawl into a bed. They know that they will be getting up
before long. Ethiopians start counting the hours of the
day at daybreak because that's when most people start
their work. Since the country is almost on the equator,
dawn comes at about the same time each morning.

Different Lifestyles in Ethiopia

Unlike Negatwa's family, most families in Ethiopia do
not live in villages. Instead, clusters of two to four houses
dot the hillsides. During the dry season, people build
houses using a large center pole surrounded by smaller
poles woven into a round or oval shape. The poles are
covered by a mud and straw mixture to form the walls.
Sometimes a room is added for donkeys and other animals,
or sometimes big animals are kept in a corral made with
tree branches. Roofs are made from long, thick grass or—
in the villages and cities—from roofing tin. People eat
simple meals, often eating meat only once every few
weeks. They farm the fields around their houses.

On the plains, people live the simplest lives of all.
Often they live in houses made from animal skins or from
river grass that can be quickly taken down and set up
again wherever their group moves. The Nuer and Anuak

tribes plant sorghum and corn. They also fish and tend cattle along the Baro River. The Mursi, Karo, and Guleb tribes roam with flocks and herds along the Omo River. Masongo hunt and gather honey in the thick rain forests of southwestern Ethiopia. Tribes like the Tishena clear fields and grow crops, mostly corn, in the southwest highlands. Some of the Afar who live in the fearful heat of the Danakil desert have settled in villages along the Awash River. Others still wander with herds of cattle— camels, cows, sheep, and goats. All of these people—and people from other rural tribes—eat very simply. Some eat a kind of corn porridge. Those who have herds do not eat much meat because they need to save their animals, but will often mix milk with animal blood.

City Life

Even fewer families live in cities. Many city families still keep animals in their compounds, but some have kitchens that are not part of the main house. Houses in the city and in some parts of the countryside may also have beehives.

In Addis Ababa, Mamoosh's family lives in a simple house that used to be a store. The family used to make money from the store, but some tough people ran them out of business. Now they live on whatever money Mamoosh brings home from odd jobs.

For years each kebele had to provide a certain number

of boys for the army. Mamoosh used to be impressed by the army literature that he read. Then his older brother joined the army. Mamoosh went to see him and discovered that soldiers fought on the front lines for fifteen days or so without food, only water. If they tried to escape or retreat without orders, they were shot. After that, Mamoosh hid in the rafters or ran out of the house when the soldiers came around.

Many families in Addis Ababa live crowded together in tiny shacks. Other families—government workers, merchants, and a few others—have enough money for a car, refrigerator, stove, television, and phone.

Wood is scarce in the city, so many people cook with kerosene instead. From time to time, there is a kerosene shortage, and people stand in line for hours to buy it. The city still smells like wood smoke, though, because people like to burn eucalyptus wood and seed pods when they can. Women go out to the countryside to buy bundles of wood from landowners. They carry the bundles into town on their backs to sell at the markato.

During the war, commercial shipping was often disrupted. People in Addis Ababa have had to put up with shortages—not only kerosene, but also butane, sugar, and even salt. But Mamoosh's mother can still buy butter, cottage cheese, baskets of red peppers and other spices, and other food in the Addis Ababa markato. Expensive downtown stores are used more by foreigners who live in

A young woman prepares a meal over a kerosene fire.

the city than by Ethiopians.

Living with War

In the north, where most of Eritrea and all of Tigre are controlled by rebel armies, war completely changed people's lives.

In Tigre, the alternative government distributed land more fairly, so farmers now manage their own land. For the first time women are being taught to plow, and have been given a voice in the political system.

Farther north in Eritrea, many men and women were

volunteer soldiers for the ELF and were never given time off from the army. They ate mostly lentils and bread and had no other clothes except their army clothes. Women served as soldiers, even commanders. Because supplies were so scarce, people developed an efficient society that found a use for things most people throw away.

During the war, people in the countryside could not put bright colored clothes outside to dry because anything bright could be used as a target for bombs. Some towns looked like ghost towns during the day because nobody lived above ground. At night, people climbed out of their underground houses to talk, cook, get water, and take care of their little gardens. Many people lived up against hills, their roofs hidden by acacia branches. Scattered throughout Eritrea were schools, hospitals, orphan camps, and factories that were underground, in caves, built against the hillside, or camouflaged in some other way.

For most people in other parts of Ethiopia, the war seemed far away. But it did affect their lives. Young men and boys were drafted to fight in the army. When the rural men were gone, women in the villages had to take care of farming while they care for their children, older relatives, and households. As the war dragged on and on, it changed the way people had lived for centuries.

7. *The Tough Job of Getting an Education*

Education in Ethiopia has traveled a long and difficult road. In the old days, priests taught a few Amhara and Tigre students to read the Psalms and Gospels in Geez. All the sons of rich families learned to read. Poor families would try to send one child—never a girl—to be educated.

In 1890, Emperor Menelik II started to introduce modern education, but little effort was put into the new system until Haile Selassie became emperor. Then, education suffered another blow. During one three-day massacre in 1937, Italian soldiers wiped out almost every educated Ethiopian in the country.

After Emperor Haile Selassie defeated the Italians and returned to his country, the task of finding teachers and setting up schools was even harder than before. But the young emperor was determined to have schools. He built and staffed one of Addis Ababa's first schools and invited people from foreign countries to help him set up others. Still, for years, once students completed high school they had to go overseas for further study. In 1950, however, Ethiopia's first university, now named Addis Ababa University, was established.

For all these improvements, university students once called Haile Selassie "father," and he met with them personally on special days. Eventually, though, educated people began to want changes in Ethiopia, and there were clashes between the university and the palace. In the 1960s and early 1970s, high school and university students criticized Haile Selassie's government with countless speeches and demonstrations. Ironically, after the revolution in 1974, idealistic students and teachers continued to criticize the new military government. This did not go unnoticed. In the time known as the red terror, 1977–1978, about a third of the university community was killed. Despite this difficult history, the country continues to tackle the tough job of providing an education for children and adults.

The Lucky Ones

Children who get to go to school in Ethiopia consider themselves the lucky ones. Even though Emperor Haile Selassie stressed education, he had trouble starting schools in remote areas. By the time of the revolution, about 93 percent of the Ethiopian people still couldn't read and write. In 1979, the new government began a national literacy campaign to teach everyone to read. More than three hundred centers were set up throughout the country, and the campaign won an award from the United Nations. For a while, before the war took the government's attention away from literacy, crowds of adults could be seen at

Because children are often needed to work on the family farm, very few are able to attend school regularly.

night walking to their classes, even in isolated areas.

Now many more Ethiopians can read and write. But education is still difficult. In the highlands, children are often needed to look after the cattle and do household and field work. In the lowlands, adults and children alike spend almost all their time tending livestock.

The war affected the schooling of many children as well because the government could not devote as much time and effort to education as it should. In areas of the north where fighting was intense, children could not go to

school at all. But in many ELF-controlled towns, most
children under twelve attended school for about three
hours a day. Along with learning to read and write,
students were never allowed to forget the importance of
their struggle for independence. In fact, most of their
teachers carried weapons to class. Orphans, cared for in
camps that were camouflaged or built into the hillside,
still went to school. Adults also attended classes. Even
soldiers studied in the trenches.

An Urban Education

In Addis Ababa, Mamoosh, who is a seventh-grade
student, rises at daybreak to get ready for school. He
doesn't eat breakfast. Sometimes he goes to church
before school. But before 8:00 A.M., he stops what he is
doing and runs to school, almost two miles (3.22 kilometers) away.

Mamoosh attends a special school that was started
with money donated by the Swedish government. Only
children with high test scores can attend. Small class size
is one of the reasons that this school is so sought after.
Ordinary classrooms have 80 to 120 students, and even
private schools have 50 to 60 to a class. But Mamoosh
studies in classes with only about 30 other students.

Most students in Ethiopia go to school for only a half
day at most, because schools generally have two or three

shifts a day. That way, more students have a chance for an education. In cities outside of Addis Ababa, some kindergarten classes have as many as four hundred students and high school classes have more than a hundred students in them. High schools have fewer students in keeping with the respect and privilege that comes with age, and high schools in Addis Ababa, where there are plenty of teachers, generally have only thirty to forty children to a class.

In the Amharic alphabet, each symbol stands for an exact sound, so a *tamari* (student) can learn to read quickly. Each character has seven different sounds, depending on which vowel is being combined with it. If you walk outside the classroom of young Ethiopian children, you will hear them all chanting their alphabet sounds together. It is the way children have learned the alphabet for centuries. Though reading is easy, writing is hard because Amharic is written with 282 different symbols. The *astamari* (teacher) emphasizes the importance of forming each character exactly right.

Mamoosh studies geography, history, Amharic, English, math, and science. Up until 1989, he had a class in political education. In 1989, the political situation changed so much that students argued with the teachers and no one knew what to teach anymore. So political education was dropped.

Mamoosh's classes last until noon. By the time he

gets home, there is often no lunch left, so Mamoosh goes off to do work. When he's not working, he plays soccer with the neighborhood boys. He used to raise pigeons with three other boys, but they gave up because too many of the birds were eaten by weasels and cats.

Mamoosh will go to school through the twelfth grade, a privilege most rural children still do not have. He would like to become a doctor when he grows up, but he thinks his dream is impossible because he says that only rich students get scores high enough to attend the university.

Grade twelve is a short year because in the middle of the year, all seniors take an important test. After the test, they no longer go to school. But the eleventh grade students plan a huge graduation ceremony for the end of the year and the twelfth graders come back to celebrate. Those with the best scores are admitted to the university.

Before 1920, girls were not allowed to go to school. In 1955, Haile Selassie's government decreed that special attention should be given to helping girls attend school, but most rural families thought education was unnecessary for girls. By the 1970s, only .6 percent of rural women could read and write. Now a girl who has a high enough score can go to the university, even become a doctor if she likes.

The main campus of Addis Ababa University is in a palace built by Haile Selassie before the Italian occupation.

After the occupation ended, the emperor donated the palace and the grounds that he had inherited from his father. A second university is in Asmara. Not everyone who gets an education after high school goes to the university, though. There are other opportunities for education.

A Church Education

Although the number of students taught by priests dropped when public schools were started, some families still choose to send their children to church schools where they study mostly in Geez. Some of those boys then choose the special and long training that will teach them to be debteras. After elementary school, they go to school to learn music and song, dance, poetry, and theology. It can take as long as seven years for a debtera to learn the collections of hymns in the first course. Learning to play rhythm instruments and to dance the church dances can take another seven years. A course in poetry comes next, for traditional Ethiopian poetry was meant to be sung.

By the time a debtera is done, he may have spent about twenty years learning music, poetry, and theology. Some debteras choose to specialize in one branch. Once his training is complete, a debtera uses his drum, sistrum, and prayer stick at every Orthodox Christian church service. There can be between twenty to forty debteras at a church during an important celebration, such as Timket. Through their dedication, debteras have preserved the music of the Orthodox church.

Education can help solve medical problems in Ethiopia, which has fewer doctors per person than any other country in the world. In the late 1980s, the Ministry of Health started a new two-year training program to educate district health managers, set up so that students can "learn by doing." They start by doing a survey of an area with government and community leaders. Then they go out to work in different communities. One of the main jobs of the new health managers has been to find safe water supplies—a big problem in rural Ethiopia.

There are also technical schools, adult training centers, and night schools where adults can learn skills. Unfortunately, not everyone who graduates can find a job.

Challenges of Rural Education

In Maji, Negatwa's children, too, go to school. But it's not always easy to get teachers to remote places like Maji. Once the government assigned a teacher who flew into Maji airfield and looked for a fancy car to drive him up the mountain. There was no car. There wasn't even a mule. The teacher had to walk. Halfway up the steep mountain, he threw up his hands and said, "They can keep the salary. I won't go up this cliff." Now the local people have named the cliff after the teacher. They call it "*yeker demosay*" *gedell* ("let my salary go" cliff).

No matter where they teach, educators all over Ethiopia have a difficult job. When schools were new, many people from other countries were recruited as staff. By 1967, all elementary and high school principals were Ethiopian. Still, rural first graders were often taught by people who had only completed the fourth grade. Now several programs provide excellent training for new teachers. But educators still struggle with classrooms where students have to sit on mud benches or even under trees, with shortages of books, and with a traditional attitude that does not respect teaching as a profession. In fact, an old proverb says that he who works with children will remain childish himself.

Educators are heartened in the face of hardships and shortages by the knowledge that the situation is improving. In 1974, only 9 percent of Ethiopia's children in grades one through six had a chance to go to school. Now, more than 50 percent, including almost all city children, are in school. As Ethiopia solves its educational problems, many of its other old problems will become easier to solve.

8. Olympic Runners and Soccer Matches

Most children in Ethiopia have no toys. But that doesn't mean they don't play. True, boys and girls have serious responsibilities at home, and children are brought up to be well-behaved and respectful. A young child is taught to obey and respect elders above all else. But children are children and they always find time to play.

Toys from Scraps

Since the country is so poor, many young Ethiopian children make toys from scraps, mud, leaves, and branches. Imitating their mothers, little girls pretend to make flour by grinding dirt between two stones. Little boys build small mud homes and pretend to plow. City children take the rims off of old barrels and run down the street rolling them like hoops. Young children also cut branches from trees, put them between their legs, and gallop as if riding a horse. Using mud, they make animals or play a game called *yeaheka teyet*, where mud is shaped over a pot until it dries and is then thrown onto the ground to explode. With different colored scraps of cloth, children or their parents or relatives make an *ashangulit*, which serves as a doll. The children gather these dolls together and play house or act out wedding ceremonies or feasts.

Children of the plains and forest work especially hard, but they still have time for play. A Tishena boy will make a *felilit* (simple flute) by shaping four holes in a tiny gourd. If a boy plays around the village he will be scolded by an elder. In the fields, though, the music of the felilit helps the elders keep track of the boys and also keeps the baboons from the corn. Children in the rain forest hunt for birds with a small bow and arrow. Or they make toys, even toy airplanes like the ones they have seen on airstrips, out of grass and thorns.

Traditional Games

A few organized games have been popular for a long time. Ganna, played usually only at Christmas, is similar to field hockey. The players try for goals, using a wooden ball and sticks on a grassy field.

Debebkosh is like hide-and-seek. One child is chosen to be chief. When the seeker hides her eyes, the chief makes sure the seeker is not peeking. While the other children hide, the seeker asks, "*Kukulu?*" If the children are not all hidden, the chief says, "*Alnegam.*" If they are, the chief says, "*Nega.*" When the seeker is looking for the children, they try to reach the chief without being caught.

Kelebosh is a game like jacks, but is played with pebbles. The child tosses a pebble in the air as you would toss a ball in jacks. Since the pebble doesn't bounce,

Raising and training pigeons is a favorite hobby of many Ethiopian children.

though, the child must pick up a second pebble (the jack) from the ground and catch the first pebble (the ball) before it hits the ground.

In the city, boys like to raise pigeons as a sport. They make up their flock by buying new pigeons or by using a tame bird to tempt an unattached bird. A new bird will follow the tame one to the flock. Then the owner plucks its longest wing feathers. By the time the feathers grow

When a ball can be found, Ethiopian children enjoy playing soccer.

back, the pigeon has learned to stay in its new home where it sleeps in a cage at night and is fed a mixture of grains by its new owner.

For children who are lucky enough to have a ball, soccer, volleyball, and basketball are all popular. If they don't have a ball, they may be able to find materials to make one from string or from plastic bags wrapped together.

Few homes have television, so adult men also entertain themselves with games. Since a person gains respect with age, a man generally considers it beneath his dignity to play a game with a child. Women are too busy with home tasks to have time for games.

One game that both children and adults play is *gebeta*, which is somewhat like backgammon. Twelve holes are made in a wooden board, stone, or the ground. Each hole is filled with four pebbles. While the rules for gebeta vary from region to region, the goal is always to capture all of your opponent's pebbles.

Guks is a sport played during Timket where men and boys act out the real wars of the old days. Horses and warriors are dressed in the finery of old battle gear. Brave fighters and other important people can wear a lion's mane headdress at guks and for war dances, as a sign of status, boldness, and courage. Riders race at full speed down the course, hurling bamboo lances at their opponents, who must protect themselves with shields.

Real soldiers in the trenches play *dama*, a kind of checkers. Ethiopian chess, somewhat different than European chess, was once popular, especially among the rich. But this tradition has faded and now chess players generally play with European rules.

Tournaments and Competitions

In cities, high school teams compete against each other in volleyball, soccer, gymnastics, and basketball. Every second year, the government sponsors a huge city-wide

A parade marks the beginning of the city-wide sports festival held in Addis Ababa every other year.

sports festival in Addis Ababa and awards trophies and prizes to the winning teams.

Soccer is a passion with Ethiopians. If someone tosses a ball to an Ethiopian boy, he will instinctively put out his foot, not his hands. Crowds fill city stadiums to watch soccer matches. Every Saturday, live soccer games from England are shown on television. In 1989, when the World Cup games were broadcast live, people found every excuse to hunt down a TV and crowd around to watch and cheer. When the Africa Cup games are played in Addis Ababa, soccer fans could not be happier.

Tennis is growing in popularity in Ethiopia, and one kebele even scraped together money and materials to build their own clay courts. But tennis equipment and athletic shoes are hard to find in Addis Ababa and can be four times as expensive as in the United States. Still, the Mitsubishi Ethiopian Open is held each December. The players compete on hard red clay courts, but they have to release some pressure from their tennis balls before they start to play. If they didn't, the balls would bounce too high because of the great difference of pressure at the eight thousand foot altitude!

Ethiopia has produced many talented long-distance runners. In the 1960 Olympics in Rome, Abebe Bikila—famed for running (and winning) races in his bare feet—won the marathon, a long and grueling race of 26 miles, 352 yards (42.2 kilometers). Four years later in Tokyo, he won again, and became the first man in history to win the Olympic marathon twice. Injuries kept him from entering again at Mexico City four years later, but another Ethiopian—Mammo Wolde—brought home the 1968 gold medal anyway, along with a silver medal for the ten thousand meter race.

Other young athletes are now training as long-distance runners. In 1988, an Ethiopian set a world record at the Rotterdam Marathon. In 1989, a twenty-four-year-old Ethiopian won the Boston Marathon. The *Washington Post* called these men and others "a remarkable second generation of Ethiopian marathon runners." But Ethiopian runners did not have a chance to show how good they were in the 1988 Olympics. Because Ethiopia's socialist government believed that the games should be sponsored by both North and South Korea, Ethiopia joined other socialist countries in boycotting the games in Seoul, South Korea. Now the runners look forward to competing in the 1992 Olympics.

Ethiopians, who get plenty of exercise at a high altitude, are very athletic. When some teenagers from Connecticut visited a home for orphans in Ethiopia that they had raised money to support, they expected to find "skinny little kids" but were surprised that the Ethiopians easily beat them in volleyball!

If you try to compete in volleyball and soccer with Ethiopian students, you may discover that you cannot keep up. But your fellow players will welcome you anyway. As you get ready for a game, someone might tell you, "*Yekena.*" The word literally means, "let it be straight for you," but is used as "good luck." You will be expected to play hard and play to win. But if you lose, people will say, "*Gid yelem.*" This means, "it has no force," and is used the same way Americans would say, "Never mind."

9. Leaving Home

On July 16, 1977, a rented safari van painted with black-and-white zebra stripes pulled through the Addis Ababa inspection point and headed toward Lake Langano, a popular camping spot. The driver was an American man. Inside were ten great-grandchildren of former emperor Haile Selassie, ages two to twenty-one. Their mothers had been imprisoned and they too would be jailed if they did not escape the new government.

The next morning, the man drove the van to a deserted part of the park and parked the car on the beach. Waves tumbling onto the sand made the only noise, for the children didn't dare make a sound. Suddenly, they heard an engine. A small airplane with masking tape all over its side to hide the numbers circled low and then landed on the sand. A second plane followed. One of the pilots jumped out and ran toward them. "Come on, quickly!" he said.

The two small planes flew the man and children to Kenya. Eventually, with help from the United Nations High Commissioner for Refugees, the children and their guardians were able to fly to Sweden. From there, they

managed to get into West Germany, the immigration
point for African refugees who want to go to the United
States. About a month after they left Ethiopia, the children
were in new homes in the United States, six with an uncle
in New York and four in California with the American
family who helped them escape.

Many Ways and Reasons for Leaving

Other Ethiopian emigrants have left the country in exciting
ways. In 1984 and 1985, Israeli planes landed secretly
near the border of Ethiopia. Airlifts, named Operation
Moses and Operation Joshua, flew thousands of black
Jews, or Falashas, to Israel. There they joined other Jews
from all over the world and are making new lives in a new
country. Committees in the United States and Israel
worked for years to get permission for other Ethiopian
Jews to emigrate to Israel. In May of 1991, Mengistu's
failing government finally agreed. Some 14,000 people
were moved in one weekend. Seats were taken out of
planes so that 500 people could be squeezed into Boeing
707 jumbo jets, and as many as 28 planes were in the air
between Ethiopia and Israel at the same time.

Not all who leave Ethiopia have such dramatic stories
to tell. But they all have reasons for leaving their homeland. Although Ethiopians love their country, many
people have become discouraged with the hard times

there. Some Ethiopians left for political reasons, some because of the war and hunger in the north, some because of religious or ethnic persecution, and others because they could not find work in Ethiopia.

While many Ethiopians are committed to staying in Ethiopia and finding solutions to the country's difficult problems, about 3.5 million Ethiopians left the country in the seventeen years after the revolution. Another 20,000 people fled to nearby Kenya after Mengistu's government fell, afraid of what changes might come next. Now almost everyone you talk to in Addis Ababa has relatives living in other countries.

People Moving Around the Horn of Africa

Before 1974, young people sometimes left Ethiopia to go to college in the United States or Europe. A few of them chose to stay in western countries. But since 1974, a flood of emigrants has poured out of Ethiopia, many of them to the neighboring countries of Sudan, Djibouti, and Somalia. In 1986, fifteen hundred Ethiopians were arriving at one refugee camp in Somalia every day.

Unfortunately, Somalia, which by 1980 had more refugees than any place else in the world, is itself a poor country. The *New York Times* reported, "The refugees' camps are squalid. There are almost no doctors, little medicine, insufficient food, few schools, no prospect of going home soon and little chance of being absorbed by their dirt-poor foster homeland."

In 1988, the U.S. Committee for Refugees reported that there were 677,000 refugees in Sudan from Ethiopia. Ironically, people from Sudan flee drought and civil war in their own country, and cross into southwestern Ethiopia.

In 1988, 265,000 Sudanese were living in relief camps on the plains of Ethiopia. Humanitarian relief organizations work to provide food, medical supplies, and clothing for people in refugee camps in both Sudan and Ethiopia. They also help resettle people in the United States and other countries.

A New Life

Once in the United States, families have hard adjustments to make. To begin with, they have to figure out ways to earn a living. Some work as professionals, while others do manual labor, and still others start small businesses. Because of Ethiopia's wonderful cuisine, a number of families run Ethiopian restaurants. People can now eat Ethiopian food in many major cities across the country.

Ethiopians carry their educational ambitions with them to the United States. Most study and work hard and learn the political system of their new country. U.S. government studies show that Ethiopians in the United States become self-sufficient quickly. The Office of

Refugee Resettlement reports that they usually find work and use fewer welfare benefits than other refugee groups.

But making a new home is still hard. Families see snow for the first time in the winter. When parents tell their American-educated sons and daughters that they went to school barefoot, their children laugh in disbelief. Young men struggle with the question of marriage. Should they marry an American woman, or can they find an Ethiopian wife? People miss their families and relatives, the beautiful Ethiopian land, and the food.

But while they struggle, Ethiopians are making cultural contributions to their adopted countries. Abiyi Ford and Haile Gerima are Ethiopian-American filmmakers. Haimanot Alemu directs the Ethiopian Theater Company, which performs plays in Amharic in the Washington, D.C. area.

Contemporary Ethiopian artists live, work, and exhibit in the United States. Writers publish books. Ethiopian scholars work as faculty members and deans in American universities. The North American Ethiopian Soccer Team Federation hosts tournaments for teams from many states and Canada. Ethiopian musicians teach people to play traditional instruments like the *krar*. They also perform with modern instruments, like the guitars and drums and keyboards played by the all-Ethiopian Dallol Band that performs with reggae star Ziggy Marley.

Many Ethiopians want to make a contribution to

Many Ethiopians are moving to the United States in search of a better life.

their homeland, even while they live away. Some
Ethiopian-Americans go to the Sudan to work in refugee
camps. Others help Ethiopian families that have just
arrived in the U.S. Still others work for political change.
In 1990, "Ethiopians for Peace and Famine Relief"
marched from Capitol Hill to the White House and sent
letters to presidents Bush and Gorbachev. "Eritreans for
Peace and Democracy" hosted a symposium in Arlington,
Virginia.

Remembering a Rich Heritage

Ethiopian families struggle to keep the parts of their
culture that are important and tell their stories and history
to their children. They also struggle with the question of
whether they want to live outside of Ethiopia forever.
Many say that they have only left temporarily. As soon as
things are better in Ethiopia, they want to return.

For some of the ethnic groups who were dominated
for centuries in Ethiopia, the adjustment is particularly
confusing. An Eritrean man, though he does not feel that
his country should be part of Ethiopia, tells Americans
that he comes from Ethiopia because, "nobody knows
where Eritrea is." Many young Oromo emigrants do not
know their own heritage. While their families were living
in Ethiopia, their parents were afraid to teach them their
Oromo roots because anyone suspected of sympathizing

with the Oromo Liberation Front would be thrown in prison.

Strong Oromo communities in Minneapolis, Washington, D.C., and Toronto have set up the "Union of Oromo in North America" and the "Oromo Relief Association," which are committed to helping Oromo youngsters understand who they are. Several Oromo groups here have made records of village and modern Oromo music. Others have formed dance troupes. The first Oromo textbooks written in Roman rather than Amharic script were printed in 1990. "Oromo School," is taught to help Oromo children learn their own language. A young girl sings, "We are a new generation of Oromos. Through my generation, our differences will be bridged."

Almost everyone who has ever lived in Ethiopia has a strong feeling for the country with its beauty, complications, its history and its people. A newsletter called *Friends of Ethiopia*, in fact, is published for Americans who lived in Ethiopia and do not want to lose touch.

If foreigners feel this way, imagine how strongly most Ethiopians feel about having to leave Ethiopia. Most miss their country very much. Many choose to work to make things better in Ethiopia or for others who leave. Though they have given much to their new homes, most talk about returning some day to put all their efforts toward building a strong, new Ethiopia.

Appendix

Ethiopian Embassies and Consulates in the United States and Canada

Consulates and embassies are happy to help you find out more about Ethiopia. Send an envelope with your name on it and two first-class stamps, and they will send you a packet of materials about Ethiopia. Or you can call or write to them with questions.

Ethiopian Embassy
2134 Kalorama Road N.W.
Washington, D.C. 20008
Phone (202) 234-2281

Ethiopian Mission to the U.N.
866 U.N. Plaza, Suite 560
New York, New York 10017
Phone (212) 421-1830

Ethiopian Embassy and Consulate
Tower B, Suite 208
112 Street
Ottawa, Ontario K1P 5P2
Phone (613) 235-6637

Glossary

Note: The Amharic alphabet has many sounds that are not used in the Roman alphabet. These may be hard for English-speaking people to pronounce. *T* and *k* are sometimes explosives, meaning that they make a clicking sound at the back of the mouth or up by the teeth. *R* is sometimes rolled. To speak Amharic properly, you do not accent any syllable. Explosives are shown here by a capital letter.

Addis Ababa (ah-dees ah-buh-bah)—new flower. Name of Ethiopia's capital.

alicha (ah-leech-ah)—vegetable stew.

alnegam (ahl-nuhg-ahm)—"they have not disappeared."

amba (ahm-bah)—a flat-topped mountain.

Amharic (ahm-hair-ak)—language of the Amhara tribe.

ashangulit (ah-shahn-guh-leet)—doll made from cloth scraps.

astamari (ahs-tah-mah-ree)—teacher.

ayezo (eye-zoh)—"don't let it seize you"; cheer up.

azmaris (ahs-mahr-eez)—musicians like the minstrels of the Middle Ages.

bagana (buh-guh-nah)—harp; probably like David's harp in the Bible.

Buhe (boo-hay)—a holiday now mostly celebrated by children.

buho (boo-hoh)—dough.

dabo colo (dah-boh coh-loh)—a popular snack.

dama (dah-mah)—a game like checkers.

debebkosh (duh-buhb-kosh)—a game like hide-and-seek.

debtera (duhb-trah)—church musician/scholars.

demera (duh-muh-rah)—pole in the middle of the Maskal bonfire.

Derg (durrg)—committee; the first decision-making council of the communist government.

Egziabeher yemari (egg-zee-ah-buh-hair yee-mah-ree)—"May God spare you"; an expression said to people who are sick.

endod (en-dod)—plant used in place of soap for cleaning clothes.

Eritrea (air-i-tray-uh)—the northern province that has fought a thirty-year war for independence.

eskista (ehs-kees-tah)—a kind of dance where the shoulders move rapidly.

Ethiopia Tikdem (Ee-tee-yoh-pyah Tik-duhm)—"Ethiopia First"; early slogan of the revolutionary government. It was meant to stress pride in the country rather than one's own region or tribe.

Falasha (fah-lah-sha)—Ethiopian Jew.

felilit (feh-li-leet)—simple flute made from a gourd.

fukura (foo-kuh-ruh)—dance performed by a warrior boasting of his deeds.

ganna (guh-nah)—Christmas; literally the field hockey game played at Christmastime.

gebeta (guh-buh-tah)—game like backgammon.

gedell (guh-dell)—cliff.

Geez (Gee-eez)—sometimes called "Ethiopian Latin." Language of the Axumite empire.

gid yelem (gid yell-uhm)—never mind; literally, "it has no force."

guks (gooks)—warrior game played at Timket.

imbi-alla (im-bee-ah-lah)—"it says 'refuse'"; it won't go or won't move.

injera (in-jehr-uh)—sour bread like a thin sponge.

inset (in-tset)—food made from false banana root.

ishi nege (ish-ee nuh-guh)—okay; tomorrow.

jihad (jee-hahd)—holy war.

kebele (Kuh-buh-lay)—urban neighborhood organization; every urban household belongs to one.

kelebosh (kuh-luh-bosh)—a game like jacks.

kerempt taba (kuhr-uhmpt tah-bah)—"it is milked dry"; rainy season has ended.

Kibre Negest (kib-uhr nuh-guhst)—*Glory of Kings*, a collection of famous literature.

kinet guad (kin-et gwahd)—cultural troupe.

koba (koh-bah)—false banana plant.

krar (kuh-rahr)—a six-stringed instrument, much like the Greek lyre.

kukulu (koo-koo-loo)—used in hide-and-seek; "are they hidden yet?"

lalibalotch (lah-li-bell-ohch)—musicians; traditionally lepers.

lesana negos (luh-sah-nuh nuh-gohs)—language of the king.

markato (mar-Kot-oh)—marketplace.

masenqo (mah-sink-oh)—one-stringed fiddle; a popular instrument.

maskal (muhs-kuhl)—name of a bright yellow daisy and a celebration of the finding of the true cross.

mesob (muh-sohb)—a large basket used as a table.

nega (nuh-gah)—"they have disappeared."

negusa negast (nuh-goo-sah nuh-guhst)—king of kings.

nug (noog)—a plant like a sunflower cultivated for its oil.

Oromifa (oh-roh-me-fah)—also Oromoissa; language of the Oromo people.

Pagame (pah-guh-may)—thirteenth month of the calendar.

shamma (shuhm-mah)—a cloak made from homespun cotton.

Shengo (shun-goh)—the National Congress, a decision-making body of the government.

shifta (shif-tah)—outlaw.

sistrum (sees-trum)—metal rattle.

tamari (tah-mah-ree)—student.

tef (Tef)—a grain like millet with a pin-head grain.

tej bet (tehj bayt)—"beer house"; place for drinking beer.

Tigrinya (tig-rin-yah)—a language spoken widely throughout Eritrea and Tigre.

Timket (tim-kuht)—Epiphany.

Tississat (tees-iss-saht)—"smoke of fire"; a waterfall of the

Blue Nile.

washint (wash-int)—flute with four holes; a popular instrument.

wat (wuht)—spicy stew.

we-et (wee-eet)—the word means "discussion"; a kind of taxi.

yazzal (yah-zahl)—commands.

yeaheka teyet (yuh-hee-kah teh-yeht)—a game of throwing dry mud on the ground to hear it explode.

yekena (yee-Kuh-nah)—good luck; literally, "let it be straight for you."

yeker demosay (yuh-kuhr deh-moh-say)—keep the salary.

zamena mesafint (zuh-muh-nah mess-ah-fint)—age of princes; a time of political disunity in Ethiopia.

zanfan (zuhn-fuhn)—Amharic word for both folk songs and dances.

Selected Bibliography

Acquaye, Alfred Allotey. *Ethiopia in Pictures*. New York: Sterling Publishing Co., 1970.

Collins, Jodie. *Codeword: Catherine*. Wheaton, Illinois: Tyndale House, 1984.

Englebert, Victor. *Camera on Africa: The World of an Ethiopian Boy*. New York: Harcourt Brace Jovanovich, 1970.

———. "The Danakil: Nomads of Ethiopia's Wasteland." *National Geographic* 137, no. 2 (February 1970).

Eskin, L. "One Teen's Struggle to End Hunger." *Scholastic Update* 121, no. 12-13 (January 27, 1989).

Firebrace, James, and Stuart Holland. *Never Kneel Down*. Trenton, New Jersey: Red Sea Press, 1985.

Gerster, Georg. "Searching Out Medieval Churches in Ethiopia's Wilds." *National Geographic* 138, no. 6 (December 1970).

Kushner, Arlene. *Falasha No More: An Ethiopian Jewish Child Comes Home*. New York: Shapolsky Publishers, 1986.

Levine, Donald. *Wax and Gold*. Chicago: University of Chicago Press, 1986.

Pankhurst, Richard. *Let's Visit Ethiopia*. London: Burke Publishing Company, 1984.

Peberdy, Max. *Tigray: Ethiopia's Untold Story*. London: Relief Society of Tigray, 1985.

Suau, Anthony. "Eritrea in Rebellion." *National Geographic* 168, no. 3 (September 1985).

Woods, Harold and Geraldine. *The Horn of Africa*. New York: Franklin Watts, 1981.

Index

About the Author

Jane Kurtz was born in Portland, Oregon, but spent her childhood in a remote Ethiopian village after her family moved there when she was three years old. She attended boarding school in Addis Ababa, and returned to the United States to attend college. Although Ms. Kurtz remains in the United States, and is now "exploring the world of the frozen north," she says, "Ethiopia is in my blood."

Ms. Kurtz lives in North Dakota with her husband and three children. She is a freelance writer of children's books, and leads several workshops.